Additional Books by Sam

Fantasy Football Guidebook: Your Cor
Playing Fantasy Football

-Named one of Top 4 Fantasy Football books of All-Time by
RotoNation.com
-Award-winning finalist in the Sports category of the National
Best Books 2008 Awards, sponsored by USA Book News
-Finalist in the Sports category of the 2009 National Indie
Excellence Awards

Fantasy Football Tips: 201 Ways to Win through Player
Rankings, Cheat Sheets and Better Drafting

Released in the summer of 2009, *Fantasy Football Tips* has become an
even bigger hit than *Fantasy Football Guidebook*, beating the one year
sales mark in only nine months of availability!

Fantasy Football Almanac: The Essential Fantasy Football
Reference Guide

The Almanac is unique in that Sam gives rankings based on
different scoring systems and roster requirements. Scoring includes
TD-only, performance and performance plus formats. Leagues with
two WRs and those with three WRs are also provided in addition to
auction values and IDP rankings. The Almanac also addresses
keeper/dynasty leagues.

Fantasy Football Almanac 2008
Fantasy Football Almanac 2009
Fantasy Football Almanac 2010

Fantasy Baseball for Beginners (Coming Oct 2010)

A book on Personal Finance (Due to be published in May 2011.)

Media Coverage

Look for Sam's expert advice and rankings in Fantasy
Football Index, Fantasy Football Pro Forecast, Fantasy
Football Draftbook and other fantasy football magazines.

Sam also participates in a weekly "Ask the Expert"
column at www.FantasyIndex.com
Also check out
www.FantasyFootballGuidebook.blogspot.com where
Sam blogs throughout the year.

Fantasy Football Basics

The Ultimate "How to" Guide for Beginners

By Sam Hendricks

Extra Point Press
Austin Texas
United States
www.XPPress.com
Library of Congress Control Number: 2009940991
ISBN: 978-0-9824286-3-4
Copyright © 2010 by Sam Hendricks
All rights reserved
Edited by Trish Hendricks
Foreword by Emil Kadlec

Visit the author at www.FFGuidebook.com

Printed in the United States of America by Lightning Source

Bulk purchases, please contact info@FFGuidebook.com

Acknowledgements

A big hug and special thanks to my publicist, editor and communications specialist, Trish Hendricks. Without her support and assistance, none of my books would be as coherent as they have been these past few years. My mother, Fannie, also gets my biggest thanks since she always encouraged me to reach for new heights and always has a smile and love that cheers me up even to this day.

To my lovely wife Birgitte, I owe everything. She completes me. Her understanding of late nights watching football and even longer nights drafting in high stakes leagues thousands of miles (and seven time zones away) constantly amazes me. However, I fear our turf wars over the family computer have just started as she introduces the world to SewDanish, her Scandinavian Textile Art company that can be found at www.SewDanish.etsy.com and her blog at www.SewDanish.blogspot.com. Let the battle begin.

An appreciative nod to my friends and colleagues who have assisted in the proof reading, sanity checking and initial editing of this book: Tom "Duck" Donalds, Richard "Sammy" Mills and John "Kuz" Kuczka. Ned "Neckless" Rudd and Charles "Tuna" Midthun spent many hours reviewing the manuscript and this book is better due to their efforts. Hopefully I can get Tom "Hog" Behnke and Dean "Smurf" Reed to play in our local league this year so they can help on future books too!

Finally, to Kirsten and Kristine, may you know a little more about Fantasy Football now.

Foreword

In the late 1950s a unique man stumbled across an idea of combining sports and board games. Wilfred Winkenbach was a creative man who owned his own tile business and later became a part owner of the AFL Oakland Raiders.

He was an absolute sports nut and loved to play board games, which was in vogue at the time. The top sports in the late 1950s were golf and baseball. Professional football, although having been in existence for decades, was still a secondary sport in popularity.

Wink came up with an idea to rate the performance of sports players along with having a group of friends play together. He would get a group of friends together and they would select players to form their own "teams." Then the friends would play against each other over a period of time using the performance system created to determine who would win.

It is unclear which sport (assuming golf is a sport) he started with first, golf or baseball. Accord to long-time Winkenbach associate Andy Mousalimas, Wink started a Fantasy baseball league in 1959 or 1960. He called it the Superior Tile Summer Invitational Home Run Tournament or "S.T. SIHRT."

To this point, no other creation of a Fantasy sport has been found that was earlier. Hence, Wilfred Winkenbach is the father of Fantasy Sports (apologies to Dan Okrent) in my opinion.

Then came Fantasy Football (FF)

It the fall of 1962 the Raiders were finishing a 16 day road trip through the east coast with the last game in New York. Now a part owner of the Raiders, Wink was thinking of ways to promote the Raiders. Sitting in his room at the Manhattan hotel (now the Milford Plaza Hotel), he met with Bill Tunnell and Scotty Stirling.

Tunnell was the Raider's Public Relations person and Stirling was with the Oakland Tribune, covering the Raiders. They decided to take the S.T. SIHRT concept and apply it to professional football. By the time they left for California that had created GOPPPL, the Greater Oakland Professional Pigskin Prognosticators League. The primary reason for the league was to promote the Oakland Raiders and the AFL.

An interesting irony here is that FF was basically created to support the NFL. The reason it is ironic is that the NFL was quite annoyed by FF for decades. In the 1980s and 1990s if you called an NFL team and said you were playing FF and wanted to know the injury status of a player, you probably would not have liked their response.

In the late 1990s the internet started its rise to prominence. Tools were becoming available to help commissioners run their leagues. These technologies helped take the popularity of FF to a completely new level.

Despite this, the NFL still considered FF a nuisance. Then again -- what else are you going to watch on Sunday?! So why should they cater to it.

There was also a concern of the NFL and television networks that FF would be confused with gambling. At one point, NFL players were told not to talk about FF or answer any question from reporters or fans about it.

Over time this concern eased. Companies started using FF in their ads. One of the earliest was Peyton Manning and Mastercard. In that particular commercial, Manning slipped in the phrase "you are on my Fantasy team" into the theme of the advertisement. The TV Networks starting incorporating FF into their Sunday Morning broadcasts. Later the networks added player scoring information into their tickers at the bottom of the screen.

Then, finally, the NFL recognized FF by starting their own commissioner service. Fantasy managers were stoked. A sense of pride and recognition was felt. Unfortunately this euphoria was perhaps misguided. Over time, it appeared the NFL was merely recognizing the opportunity to make money on the phenomena called FF and not necessarily supporting the Fantasy manager with a broadcast tailored to their needs.

The Commissioner Evolution

In the beginning, the commissioner had a heavy load when it came to the league's needs. All the stats had to be gleaned from the newspaper. Many commissioners did results by hand in the early days. Then came spreadsheets and word processors to make the presentation slicker. Weekly results were printed on a dot matrix printer and mailed out to all the managers each week.

Then in the 1980s software tools became available. These, of course, were crude compared to today's standards. You first loaded the software on your computer. Each week you downloaded the week's player stats off of what I remember as a bulletin board over a phone connection. There was a point in the late 80s and early 90s when "phone team management" became the big deal. You could use the touch-tone to make roster changes and set starting lineups each week. This was so important in the pre-internet days there was a legal patent squabble. The man who first saved Fantasy sports from patent chaos was Paul Paulsen. He owned Fantasy City and fought a patent challenge on phone systems in Fantasy sports, arguing it was already in public use. Paul was successful and Fantasy sports continue to grow. Paul is gone now, and I wish we had documented better all he did for the industry.

The internet, of course, opened up a whole new market for tools to run your leagues. This has made commissioning much easier and helped bring a greater participation to the hobby.

Contests

Although national leagues and contests were available back in the 1980s, the internet gave them a big boost. CDM was one of the first and featured salary cap type leagues. These leagues did not require any type of drafting which was very important in the pre-internet days.

High Stakes
The hobby took another step in 2002 with the introduction of the World Championship of Fantasy Football. This event broke the sound barrier of Fantasy sports managers' trust in companies. Despite the hobby being over 40 years old, the public was still unsure about handing a company a large amount of money and expecting it to be there at the end of the Fantasy year. Included in their concern was the internet in general when dealing with money and accurate and reliable performance of a large "Money league."

Back to the Future
The information age has exploded. More timely information is accessible now then ever before. Injury information, weekly forecasts, etc are available during the regular season. Also Draft Strategy knowledge was in its early stages of growth. As player information became better, drafting strategy was more important then ever. Having a firm basic understanding of how to draft is essential today. This knowledge and ability is now the new frontier. The Fantasy managers understanding and execution of drafting strategy can make the biggest difference in their success.

I first met Sam at the World Championship of Fantasy Football (WCOFF) and was impressed by his knowledge. The WCOFF includes an elite group of Fantasy Football talent. The competition is fierce. After reviewing his book published at that time, "Fantasy Football Guidebook", I was glad Sam was not in my league. He has a great understanding of Fantasy Football and writes it in a very readable and understanding format.

Fantasy Football Basics
Sam has done a great job enlightening us with details on a broad range of important topics that are important to not only the beginner but the seasoned veteran too.

The beginner will enjoy chapters 1, 2 and 3 to learn some of the pros and cons about FF. Why you should play and the many ways you can play.

Chapter 4 is where all skill level FF managers can learn. How to deal with roster sizes, free agency and trades are some of the must read topics. These are important concepts that can get you into the playoff. The draft is the highlight but winning requires an excellent understand of these topics.

Skipping ahead to chapters 7 and 8, you will find details on drafting. The draft is the most talked about and thought out part of FF -- and it should be.

In-season management, if often overlooked, is a fundamental attribute to succeeding at FF. Chapters 9, 10 and 11 provide the juicy details that can turn an average drafted team into a playoff contender.

Enjoy this book! It is an excellent source for the beginner and the seasoned veteran Fantasy Footballer. You can never stop learning to become a better manager and this book is a great help.

Emil Kadlec
Owner _FootballDiehards.com_
May 2010

Table of Contents

Chapter 1 Why play Fantasy Football?

I have written this book as a simple, straightforward "guide" on how to play fantasy football. This book is a great gift for anyone who is just getting started or thinking about playing fantasy football. _Fantasy Football Basics_ is also great for anyone (parents, spouses, youngsters, etc.) interested in learning more about the game

In your hands is an easy, step-by-step guide for beginners on how to play fantasy football. I promise there will be no jumping around from front to back to middle. Just read this straight through to get the basics. I have tried to write this in a non-insulting (demeaning) manner. There are no pictures, no cute diagrams and hopefully, no condescending language. I do not want you to feel discouraged or stupid simply because you have questions about a hobby that 30 million other people play. In fact, when I did a focus group to test the title for this book, some of the feedback was that some titles made people feel bad about getting certain help books. I have intentionally tried to go out of my way to _NOT_ embarrass you or make you feel dumb.

The order of the book is designed to immerse you in fantasy football slowly and from the beginning. I am using the tried and true teaching method of "tell them what you want them to know and then give them a summary of what you told them." I am not going to repeat myself three times in each chapter. Important stuff is in bold and a summary is provided at the end of most chapters for those who like a little cheat sheet.

We will start with why you may want to play fantasy football and what is football and fantasy football; then cover their history and where to start. The next two chapters cover the rules (hint there are no official rules but there are some standard ones that many leagues use) and scoring systems; both chapters are critical to playing well. Chapter 6 covers ranking players and is more of a reference for qualities and trends at these point scoring positions, but it is the perfect lead in to Chapter 7 - Drafts, which provides draft preparation tips. But how do you know who to pick at the draft? Chapter 8 covers preparing for the draft including two stratgeies (one easy and one hard). Once you have your players, what do you do with them? Chapters 9, 10 and 11 discuss which players to start each week and how to acquire other players. Chapter 12 provides additional tips for those fantasy owners fortunate enough to qualify for the fantasy playoffs. Finally, the last two chapters give resources (books, magazines and websites) and some miscellaneous words of wisdom.

I follow the KISS (Keep It Simple Sam) principle-

Steps to playing FF

1) Pick/Join a league (Ch 3-5)
2) Prepare for the draft (Ch 6 and 8)
3) Draft your team (Ch 7)
4) Make weekly roster decisions (Ch 9)
5) Improve your team (Ch 10 and 11)

I do not mean to presume that all fantasy football players are male, but recent studies show that as many as 90% of today's players are men, so I will use the male pronouns throughout this book, but it is written with no gender in mind. You will find no off-color jokes, no sexist remarks and no profanity here. Any person, male or female, young or old, can learn about fantasy football and not feel intimidated or chastised.

By the same token, I will use the abbreviation FF for fantasy football from now on. Paper is a valuable resource (think trees…OK, money). So, rather than waste space and money spelling out fantasy football each time I refer to it, I will simply write FF. I will refer to players on your team and this includes a team defense as well, but I will not mention defense every time in reference to players on your team.

Finally, throughout this book I will use the term "owner" to mean you, the fantasy football player, since you are, in effect, the owner, manager and coach. If I say "player" it is in reference to a football player or athlete who plays or should eventually play NFL football. I will use the term coach for NFC head coaches unless otherwise mentioned.

There are some common FF/NFL terms and acronyms, which you should familarize yourself with in the container below:

QB	=Quarterback
RB	=Running Back
WR	=Wide Receiver
TE	=Tight End
K	=Kicker
DEF	=Defense
ST	=Special Teams
TO	=Turnover (Fumble or Interception)
HC	=Handcuff (Drafting a player's backup)
IDP	=Individual Defensive Player
TD	=Touchdown
XP	=Extra Point
FG	=Field Goal
FP	=Fantasy Points (based on player's stats and scoring system of league)
PPR	=Points per Reception
OL	=Offensive Line
NFL	=National Football League
REC	=Reception or catch of a pass
YPC	=Yards per Catch

You will also see some common notations for player rankings and draft spots. Rankings are annotated after the position abbreviation so the 12th best RB will be RB12. The #1 WR on a team will be WR1. The last ranked defense in the NFL will be DEF32. Draft spots are denoted by round and then the spot within the round after a decimal. So the first pick of the first round is 1.01. The 12th pick of the second round is 2.12. Therefore, we can have RB25 drafted in the third round with the fifth pick (3.05)

I believe that 80% of the FF production can come from 20% of the work. This is known as the 80/20 rule of FF. The key is knowing what 20% to do and…deciding if the other 20% performance from 80% more work is worth it. I intend to show you that with my easy and hard way. The easy way is just that…easy.

Will it win you a championship? It may or it may not. The hard way takes more effort and work but generally results in better production. (If that extra effort is worth it to you –you be the judge).

Woody Allen is quoted as saying, "80 percent of success is just showing up." The same thing can be said for FF. If you attend the draft (versus getting someone else to draft for you), you will have a better team. Putting in 30 minutes of effort before the first game of the week and setting your lineup week in and week out will prevent many FF mistakes in roster management. Reading the notes provided by your league website about your fantasy players can stop a season-ending error. All of these things are easy and not too time consuming. They are the FF equivalent of "just showing up." Do these things and 80% success is yours.

I was lucky enough to fly RF-4s and F-15E fighter jets in my Air Force career. Fighter pilots do not have time to debate all of the possibilities when flying at 600 miles an hour or at 300 feet off the ground. They need hard and fast rules to follow and a method for quickly determining the right choice. Fighter pilots use checklists and that is what I am about to provide you. You will find checklists for how to pick a league, how to rank players, and how to decide who to start. Checklists provide you with 80% success for only 20% of the work.

If you are reading this book and you have played fantasy football for more than five years - STOP NOW! If you have won cold hard cash playing fantasy football -STOP READING! If you have won a League Championship, put the book down and run away now. You have bought, been given or are thinking about buying a starters manual for playing fantasy football. In all of the above cases, you do not need this book.

You may wish to purchase one of my other books, however, which are for more intermediate or advanced fantasy football players. My first book, _Fantasy Football Guidebook: Your Comprehensive Guide to Playing Fantasy Football,_ has done quite well (a second edition came out in March 2010) and is often referred to as the "encyclopedia of fantasy football." It is 400+ pages of information and is for the more advanced fantasy football player. It is all-inclusive, but many times people ask for just my personal tips on fantasy football. That is why I published _Fantasy Football Tips: 201 Ways to Win through Player Rankings, Cheat Sheets and Better Drafting_. _Fantasy Football Tips_ is for the fantasy football player who wants to know the best tips. It really is the best of the best.

Whether you are a newbie who wants to learn what everyone (and I mean everyone) is talking about or a casual player who wants to know more about the game, this book is for you. Options, options, options, there are so many. I will get you through it.

Anyone will be able to find exceptions to this book and pick things apart with "my league does this" and "my league does that." Just remember: The answer to many questions is "it depends." It usually depends on your scoring system or rules, or both. Sometimes it will depend on your willingness to take a risk.

And no matter why you start (whether it be a local work league or a way to stay in touch with old friends or reconnect with a child), once you start, I guarantee you will be hooked. Don't say I didn't warn you!

Fantasy Football Basics is meant to be clean, simple and functional. No cute cartoons or complicated charts or diagrams - just easy to implement ideas, checklists and rules to follow. You be the judge if I suceeded. Good luck and, as always, drop me a line or a question at info@FFGuidebook.com

Chapter 2 What is Football and Fantasy Football?

NFL

Before anyone can begin to learn about fantasy football, they need to have a basic understanding of National Football League football. If you already have a good grasp of football, skip ahead to "what is fantasy football."

In general, most FF leagues use the NFL as their basis. The NFL consists of two conferences: the American Football Conference (AFC) and the National Football Conference (NFC). Each conference has 16 teams in four divisions (4 teams each in a North, South, East and West division). These 32 NFL teams play a 16 game schedule where they play each team in their division twice (one game at home and one away game at the other team's stadium: so six games) and play a division in their conference and one outside their conference. Their two remaining games are intra-conference games based on the previous year's standing (i.e a first place finish means you play two of the other three first place finishing teams in your conference). The NFL regular season lasts for 17 weeks because each team gets one week off (a bye week) during the season. **These bye weeks occur in weeks 4-10 with anywhere from two to eight teams off in any given week.** This fact is important to FF owners.

In football, each team has 11 players on the field playing against each other. The playing field is 100 yards long with each team's end zone at the end of the field. The "red zone" is the last 20 yards on either end of the field. This zone is not actually marked on the game field but is more of a term used by broadcasters and football aficionados. The goal line is the white line separating the playing field from the end zone.

The object is to score as many points as possible in each of the four 15 minute quarters allotted to each game. The first half of the game consists of the 1st and 2nd quarters after which there is a break called half-time. This is when the band and cheerleaders perform, and it is called the half-time show. The second half consists of the 3rd and 4th quarters. If the score is tied after 60 minutes of play, then a 15-minute overtime is played, and the team that scores first is the winner.

The team with possession of the football (the team that receives the kickoff) has four downs in which to go 10 yards or more. Every time a team goes for 10 yards or more, they get a new set of downs. Teams can run or pass the ball in their attempt at achieving 10 or more yards. Generally, teams will run on first and second down, and then pass on third down, especially if they have a long way to go to get a first down (5 yards or more). Of course, there are exceptions to every rule and some teams pass much more often (NO and IND come to mind) while others run more often (BAL and MIN). Normally teams are risk averse and therefore elect to kick the ball far away on their fourth (and last, if unsuccessful) down rather than risk turning the ball over to the other team. This act of kicking the ball away to the other team on fourth down is called a punt.

Scoring occurs when a team takes the football into their opponent's end zone (or across their opponent's goal line). This is called a touchdown (TD) and teams are awarded 6 points. After a TD, the scoring team is given another play from the 2-yard line in which to try to score again. If they kick the football through the goal post it counts as one more point called an extra point (XP); if they run or pass the ball into the end zone again, it is worth two points (called a two-point conversion).

If a team faces fourth down, they can elect to try to kick the ball through their opponent's goal posts. If they are successful, they earn 3 points. This is called a field goal (FG). One other scoring method can occur. This is a defensive score called a safety. If the opponent's defense tackles the ball carrier in their own end zone, the defense scores a safety and gets two points. **Therefore, NFL scoring consists of TDs, XPs, FGs and safeties.** This is important to FF owners.

Once a team scores through a TD or FG, they kick the football to the other team (called a "kickoff") with their special teams unit. This same kickoff occurs at the beginning of each half (the team that received the kickoff in the first half has to kickoff to the other team at the start of the second half).

There are three main categories of players: offense (OFF), defense (DEF) and special teams (ST). ST consists of players on the kickoff or punt return units. The offensive players on the field consist of a QB, 1-2 RBs, 2-4 WRs, 1-2 TEs and five offensive linemen (OL).

Defenses usually run a 3-4 or 4-3 with the first number representing the amount of defensive linemen (DL) and the second number representing the number of linebackers (LB). Think of DLs as the first line of a defense and LBs as the second line of defense. The remaining four defenders (seven DL and LB, and 11 total leaves four others) are safeties or cornerbacks (usually two each). These men are the last line of defense.

So who scores all of the offensive points? QBs are the generals of the field and usually hand off the football to RBs or throw passes to the receivers. QBs throw for lots of passing yards and passing TDs. RBs can catch passes, carry the ball on running plays and even occasionally throw a pass on "trick" plays. Generally, RBs score rushing TDs and have mainly rushing yards. Some are good pass catchers too (this makes them more valuable in some leagues). WRs catch passes, have receiving yards and receiving TDs. TEs are the weak sister of receivers. They usually have less catches, yards and TDs since they sometimes stay in to block and are not the speedsters with breakaway speed that some WRs are.

So now you know a little about the NFL. But what is FF?

What is Fantasy Football?

You may have heard your co-workers talking about it in the office last year or your son is interested in playing this year with his school friends. In any case, you need to know what is so magical about this thing called FF. Everyone seems to be involved with it, but you just do not get it.

More than 30 million people play FF, so something must be special about it. You may have heard vague references to a "draft" and "players" on a team and not starting the right player. Don't fret all will be revealed.

Basically it is a game of "I am better than you are" at NFL knowledge. I know more about who is going to do well (score) than you... But how does one decide who is the better football aficionado or expert? You and I might decide to pick players from each primary scoring position (QB, RB, WR, TE and Kicker) and then see which "team" does the best over the season.

How do we measure success? By who scores the most TDs and gains the most yardage. However, QBs have (throw) more TDs than RBs or WRs in a season. So passing TDs will be worth less than rushing or receiving TDs. The same can be said for yards. QBs throw for over 200 yards in many games; RBs and WRs are doing great if they get 100 yards. So, passing yards need to be valued about half as much as rushing/receiving yards.

In that case, you may rightly point out a foul if one or more of your players becomes suspended and is out for the season. "That's not fair!" you cry; "I should at least get a chance to replace my suspended players just as they do in the NFL". Therefore, we change our little contest and allow FF "owners" to drop players and add new ones. The next point of contention is if some of my RBs are dinged up for a few weeks and thus drag my RB average down because they do not score or get yards when they are injured. In this case, we modify the rules and only start a limited number from each position so that "owners" can decide which players they expect to perform the best. In fact, we decide to make it just like the NFL, where 1 QB, 2 RBs, 2 WRs, 1 TE and 1 Kicker start each week.

Now take our two-owner contest and expand it to eight to twelve other co-workers, friends or relatives who think they know more than we do and you have a league. Before the season starts, the league has a draft to determine which owner gets which players. This is usually a lively afternoon of fun where owners get to look each other in the eye and puff up their chests about how smart they are. Owners take turns picking players who are then exclusively on just their team, (i.e. Peyton Manning can only be on one team in the league). The rules determine how many total players are on each team, how many players from each position must start each week, and how each player scores.

There is a great sense of pride in putting together your "hand-picked" team and coaching them to a championship; especially when it means beating your friends and neighbors. In fantasy football, you are the owner, general manager (GM) and coach of a team of NFL players. Complete with all the decisions that go with it, but without the millions of dollars it would cost.

Here is how it works. You name your team and then in a draft, just like in the NFL, you get to pick players to fill your roster. Each week you will decide who to start and who to bench. As the owners, you can make trades with other teams (if they agree) or drop players who are not performing and pick up others from a free agent pool (players not drafted in the draft or dropped by another owner). Your objective is to have the best regular season record (by winning each week), advance to the fantasy football playoffs and, eventually, win the FF Super Bowl. Throughout it all, the experience is a major ego trip since you drafted them, you own them and you determined who would play or start for the week.

How much time will it take? Fantasy football is a pursuit that takes as little or as much time as you want to give it. I have friends that I have introduced to the game who become very engaged (read obsessed) and devote many hours trying to get an edge. I have other friends that spend an hour or so before the games begin for the week and use that time to set a lineup. The most fun comes in the bragging rights of knowing you met your opponent in a head-to-head matchup and came out with a victory. Remember, the winner of the fantasy football Super Bowl will have a year's worth of bragging rights.

What is the attraction of fantasy football? I am asked this all the time! So I came up with the Top 10 reasons to play FF. Hopefully, you can find one for you.

Top 10 Reasons to Play Fantasy Football

1) You want to affect the outcome of a football game in a way you never could before.

2) Competition with other football fans. Players enjoy the opportunity to match their skills against co-workers, friends, and family members. One survey reports that 3 out of 4 fantasy sports participants play with others they know personally. Most men are competitive and this allows us to compete without getting off the couch.

3) You love to watch football and your favorite team is driving you crazy.

4) The social aspect of belonging to a group appeals to some; not to mention social networking or sharing a hobby with your children or spouse.

5) Fantasy football gives you one more reason to cry, laugh, yell, scream, rant or jump for joy while watching NFL football. It is like gambling but without the guilt.

6) Fantasy football makes for better NFL fans. We are more educated about the nuances. We are more aware of the player's skill sets. We care about the rules and the changes each year brings. We are more attuned to the NFL.

7) Fantasy football helps you appreciate all the talent in the NFL, not just the talent on your favorite team.

8) Sometimes you watch a game to see how one or more of your players will do. Other times it is to see how your opponent's player does. Still other times it is to see how a player you are considering adding to your team is doing. Bottom line, you watch more and different games.

9) It prevents you from having to cut the grass on Sundays.

10) You want to win, have fun and have something to brag about around the water cooler at work (or at family gatherings). It is for the adrenaline rush of winning.

Why are Fantasy Footballers so Committed to the Game?

The reason fantasy football is the most popular fantasy sport is because it is played once a week and every game counts. In fantasy baseball, hockey or basketball, you can have over 100 games, so you have a situation where the games do not have that much meaning. In fantasy football, it is all about Sunday games or Monday night. Instant gratification lets you enjoy it for a few hours. Another reason might be that the games restore a feeling of ownership that slipped away from many fans with the advent of free agency. Now you can draft players and in some leagues (Keeper Leagues) you can keep most of your team (players) together through the years.

What are the Arguments Against Fantasy Football?

1) Fantasy football is gambling. Oh my! If a hobby that asks for an entry fee (to pay for the costs of running the thing) and gives a few baubles (bucks) back (and maybe a trophy) to the winner is gambling, then so is golf, bowling, bridge, and so on. Gambling should be where everyone has an equal chance of winning. Fantasy football is not a place where everyone has an equal chance of winning. You win by preparation, some luck, skillful drafting and season transactions. Gamblers play against the house. Fantasy football players play against their friends. In fact, Congress declared FF was not gambling with their 2006 legislation (see History of FF later in this chapter).

2) It takes up too much time. Actually, it will only take as much time as you want to put into it. If the family wants to go to Wally World on Sunday, take them. Just make sure you tape the games so you can watch them when you get home. And do not leave the house until your lineup is set. Don't worry, I will provide you with easy steps to minimize the time spent.

So I ask again, what is fantasy football? It is a way to enjoy the game of football on a higher level. It is a method of competing while watching the sport you love. It is also a hugely popular social event. Anyone who has ever attended a draft knows the camaraderie and excitement of this one day of the year. It will be something to look forward to year after year. It is Christmas in August. It is about using your brain to best your friends in a challenging, yet non-threatening way. It is about getting together, laughing at other's picks, sharing outrage as your pick is snatched from you and looking forward to the upcoming season with optimism. It is the ultimate extension of the football season.

History of Fantasy Football

According to NFL.com, FF got its start on a rainy October night in 1962, when Wilfred "Bill" Winkenbach, Scotty Sterling and Bill Tunnell became the founding fathers of FF. They were relaxing and having some cocktails in a Manhattan Hotel, (now the Milford

Plaza), as the eventual 1-13 Oakland Raiders finished up a three-game, 16-day East Coast road trip (Boston, Buffalo and finally New York). This is where the rules began. They created a set of rules in which individuals could draft skill players from professional teams and play weekly games against their friends. Fantasy football was born. Of course, no great event is completed in a single session and the three men got together with George Ross, an Oakland Tribune sports editor, once they returned to Oakland and fine-tuned the draft rules.

Greater Oakland Professional Pigskin Prognosticators League (GOPPPL)

Their league was called the GOPPPL, The Greater Oakland Professional Pigskin Prognosticators League. Try saying that three times fast! There were four others who would play the next year (1963), to bring the total to eight team owners. Many of the owners took on partners or coaches. For instance, George Glace grabbed 24-year-old Ron Wolfe (former Green Bay GM) as his co-owner.

The first draft was held in Winkenbach's basement, known as Winkenbach's Rumpus room. Other drafts and playoff dinners (at the end of the season to award prizes) were held at local restaurants. Bill Winkenbach served as the first commissioner of FF, and as such he prepared weekly reports that were delivered to each GOPPPL owner on the Tuesday morning of each game week.

Andy Mousalimas collaborated with Scotty Sterling and later opened up the Kings X Sports bar in 1968. The first Kings X draft was held in 1969. There was only one division then, but it soon grew to five divisions by 1972. No women were allowed to play at that time, but in 1974, Al Santini suggested an all-women's division and the Queens division began. This marks one of the first written documentations of women and fantasy football. By 1974 the game had over 200 participants.

Word spread about this new game. Individuals would call and request the rules. However, many groups faltered because of the cumbersome and time-consuming act of scoring. Remember, there were no Yahoo leagues to provide instant totals or to keep track of all the statistics.

The rosters had to be submitted in person on Friday by midnight (except for Thanksgiving, when the deadline was Wednesday at midnight). No changes could be made before kickoff or after Saturday's injury report. Many of the owners came to watch the Sunday games at the Kings X bar and cheered their own fantasy players, not NFL teams, causing some confusion. Sunday scores were posted Monday at lunchtime and Monday Night Football packed in the crowds. Tuesday lunch became standings day. The scoring was done manually, of course, with one person scouring the sports page with paper and pencil. Let me reiterate: there was no internet; no sports talk radio and no fantasy football magazines or books. This probably explains why the sport did not catch on immediately. Many were intimidated or simply turned off by the amount of number crunching that was involved in transforming the box scores on Monday's sports section into league scores and standings.

The computer made calculations easier. As software became available, interest increased. The internet (thank you, Al Gore) proved to be the big catalyst that propelled FF into fame. The internet took FF from sports bars and office lounges into individual homes and turned the hobby into a money-making enterprise. Today, fantasy football is big business.

Next came high-speed internet, live scoring and real time stats, so that an owner could instantly see how his team was doing against his opponent instantly. Fantasy football has progressed from small local leagues that used paper, pencil and the Monday box scores to automated websites that give you live scoring. What started as four to eight guys getting together in a basement in Oakland, has become an international phenomenon with players and leagues across the globe.

Timeline for Fantasy Football History

1962 – Fantasy Football rules born in NYC hotel room

1963 – First league formed, the GOPPPL

1969 – First Kings X Fantasy Football leagues formed

-----------------------1970-1979---

1974 – First known Ladies Division (QUEENS) at Kings X Bar

-----------------------1980-1989---

1987 – "Fantasy Football Index" Magazine first published

-----------------------1990-1999---

1990 – "Fantasy Pro Forecast" Magazine first published

1990 – The World Wide Web debuts as a new interface for the internet

1990-1999 Rapid growth due to the internet

-----------------------2000-2009---

2002 – The World Championship of Fantasy Football (WCOFF) begins

2004 – The National Championship of Fantasy Football (NFFC) begins

2006 – The Anti-gambling bill has fantasy sports carve out language. It says that fantasy games are exempt from the gambling law as long as they meet two requirements:

1) Awards and prizes must be stated prior to game starting and not be determined by number of particiapants or total entry fee revenue

2) Winning outcomes are determined by skill for contests that use results from multiple real life games

In essence, it solidifies the fact that fantasy sports are games of skill, not luck

2007 - Fantasy Football Guidebook and Fantasy Football Almanac published

2008 - Fantasy Football Players Championship begins

2009 - Fantasy Football Tips published

-----------------------2010+---

2010 - Fantasy Football Basics published

Chapter 3 Where do I start?

You may not have a choice. If you have been invited to play with friends, relatives or co-workers, then you have no say in what type of league you join, since it is already formed and waiting for you to jump in. If you said yes then the best you can do is learn from this chapter about how to play in your new FF league. For other readers, you may not be committed to any league yet. If this is the case, read on carefully and decide which type of league you will enjoy the most. My recommendations are highlighted in bold type and repeated in the chapter summary.

When I say "Avoid," it means to try not to play in such a league or follow that strategy. Notice I do not say "Never." I know it is hard to find the perfect league. I have been trying for 20 years now. In some cases, you will not have any choice in the league rules (if you were asked to join a local league). If so, just keep these thoughts in mind when it comes time to propose rule changes or if deciding on another league.

Free or Pay

Your first choice is this - Do you want to spend any of your hard-earned cash playing FF? Some leagues are free to play. Some charge a small administrative fee to pay for leagues expenses like the website, draft board, trophy and management firm that calculates the league statistics. Other leagues charge an entry fee so that they can award prizes (like a coffee mug, cash or even a ring).

If this is your first year in FF, I suggest keeping it simple and playing only in a free league or small administrative fee league. If you play in a pay league, make sure the fee is appropriate for the services provided. $15 should be more than enough to cover administrative costs. I do not recommend playing in a cash prize league when you are just starting out. Once you have a few years under your belt and feel more confident, then you can start putting your money where your mouth is. There is one large problem with free leagues - apathy. In many of these leagues the owners who are not in contention will quit on their teams. So you get what you pay for. Leagues where some prizes are involved tend to have more owner involvement. Free leagues …well, owners lose interest if they are not in the running to win late in the season. This is very frustrating, especially to a beginner who wants to play competitively. You were warned.

Here are some sites where you can join a free FF league

Yahoo (http://yahoo.com),

ESPN (http://ESPN.com)

CBSSportsline (http://CBSSportsline.com)

These sites, and even the NFL site itself (http://NFL.com), offer free FF games, many of which are tailored to the beginner. Other books go into more detail about each of these free leagues. For example, of the free leagues Martin Signore and _Fantasy Football for Dummies_ covers three well and Randy Giminez covers CBSSportsline leagues in detail.

Cash prize leagues or "money leagues" can be found in many of the same places as the free leagues, but they are run as private leagues (see below). Entry is gained by paying the entry fee. Be wary of these leagues if you do not know the commissioner (the person running the league).

There are low stakes money leagues, medium stakes leagues and high stakes leagues. I categorize the low money leagues as less than $100 for the entry fee. Medium stakes leagues are $100-$999 entry fees and high stakes leagues cost at least $1,000 to play ($2,000 for the WCOFF).

Each of the high stakes leagues have satellite leagues where you can play for around $200 or less. The FFPC even has some leagues for $77 - a great way to play for some cash but not go overboard. Seven is a "magic number" in football-it equates to a TD.

I prefer to play in well-established leagues run by professionals such as the small satellite leagues from:

1) Fantasy Football Players Championship (FFPC) (http://theFFPC.com),

2) National Fantasy Football Championship (NFFC) (www.fantasyfootballchampionship.com)

3) World Championship of Fantasy Football (WCOFF) (http://wcoff.com).

Public or Private

Your next choice is public or private. Public leagues are available to everyone and can be found at major websites such as the ones mentioned previously. **I recommend a public league unless you have been invited to join a private league where you know some of the players or the commissioner.**

Entry into private leagues can only be gained through the approval of the commissioner (the owner running the league). This may be an invite-only league where only co-workers, friends or relatives are invited or it may be only for certain types of players (for example women only, Dallas Cowboys fans or those wishing to play for cash prizes).

Along the same lines as choosing a public or private league, there is a choice between playing in a local or a national league. A local league is one run by someone you know that involves people bound together by some bond (work, school, neighborhood, relatives). Whereas a national contest like the FFPC, WCOFF, NFFC, or their satellites involve owners from all walks of life and all over the world simply playing to win money and be the best.

Head to Head (H2H) or Total Points (TP)

Now that you have decided on some of the other variables, you need to decide on the format for competing. H2H is where each owner plays another owner each week and the team with the most fantasy points that week gets a win. A total points league does not involve owners playing each other; instead, the standings are based on whichever team scores the most points. The team with the most points during the season is at the top of the standings. H2H can be more exciting as it is always fun to beat someone else. However, the schedule (who you play and when) can affect outcomes. Total point (TP) leagues, tend to be fairer, but offer less excitement. Therefore, it is a trade off. **Either format is appropiate for beginners but H2H provides more competition (hence fun).**

Draft type: Traditional or Auction

The traditional draft is sometimes called a serpentine draft since it reverses order every round, much like a snake doubling back on itself. In a traditional draft with a 12-team league, the first round goes in order 1 through 12, the second round then reverses as the 12th team gets to draft first and the 1st team (from round one) will draft last. Therefore, a five round draft would look like this:

Round 1: 1-12
Round 2: 12-1
Round 3: 1-12
Round 4: 12-1
Round 5: 1-12

Every odd numbered round (1st, 3rd, 5th and so on) has the order going from the team with the first 1st pick to the team with the 12th pick. Every even numbered round (2nd, 4th, 6th ,etc.) will have the team with the 12th pick drafting first, then the 11th pick and so on until the 1st pick drafts last.

There are some disadvantages with this traditional draft format. If you have a later draft spot, you are not afforded an opportunity early to draft the most wanted players. If everyone agrees that Adrian Peterson (RB, Minnesota Vikings) is the most desirable player, there is little hope of him being available to later drafters, since the first or second owner drafting will inevitably draft him. However, since the draft "snakes," an owner with a later draft spot does get two picks before the owner with the higher draft spot gets his second pick, thus compensating them somewhat for their late start. The 12th spot has as much as a 5% disadvantage from the 1st spot and therefore I advocate alternatives to the traditional draft. For a detailed discussion of these alternate drafts see _Fantasy Football Guidebook_.

An auction draft removes the biases of draft spot inequality. However, there are so few opportunities to participate in an auction draft that the default is a traditional draft. In an auction draft, owners start with a hypothetical budget with which to "buy" players at a player auction. Typically, $200 is used. The owner that bids the most for a given player is awarded that player and his budget is reduced by that amount. Unlike the traditional draft, every owner has the same chance to acquire every player if they wish to spend the money on them. The advantages of the auction system in removing any draft spot bias are offset by the additional time it may take for an auction draft and the "fear" of doing an untraditional draft. This is why so few FF players play in an auction league. **Due to the complexities of an auction draft, I recommend beginners play in traditional draft leagues.**

Number of Teams (8, 10, 12, 14, or 16)

An even number of teams is desirable if in a H2H league. If you have an odd number, then one team will be without an opponent every week. An odd number of teams can be fixed by using a total points (versus a H2H) system, or by averaging the scores for all teams and having the bye week team play against that average.

Most leagues consist of 8-14 teams. Some do have 16, but this is stretching it. When you begin to consider 16 teams, take into consideration the amount of players drafted and the limited supply of certain positions (QB, K, DEF) with only 32 NFL teams (see Appendix A). If your league will have 16 teams and requires each team to own two QBs, Ks and DEFs, then there will be none available to pick up in free agency. The H2H schedule is a nightmare to try to get every team a matchup with every other team. On the opposite end of the spectrum, you can form or play in a league with only eight teams, but these are too small to be competitive. In 8-team leagues, everyone has great QBs and RBs, so it is less about skill in drafting and more about luck as to who gets hurt or escapes injuries. Ten teams is, realistically, the minimum number of teams.

Most 10-team leagues use two divisions of five teams and a 14-game regular season with four teams making the playoffs. 12 or 14-team leagues are the best fit. 12-team leagues (with 3 divisions) are perfect for 14-game regular seasons, with each team playing its division opponents twice. The playoffs occur in week 15, with four teams (3 division winners and a wild card team).With 14-team leagues, you would have a 13-game regular season with six or seven teams making the playoffs (one or two teams get byes), and the playoffs last through week 16's Super Bowl.

More teams means less players available in free agency, which means a harder league. More teams also mean more money for the prize, but more competition. **For these reasons, I recommend a 10 or 12-team league for beginners. Avoid 8 or 16-team leagues. The former is too easy and the latter could be too hard for beginners.**

Skill Level

Often a league will be targeted towards a certain skill level. This is described as beginner, intermediate or experienced owners. **If you are a beginner, start in the easiest league you can find, as far as the other owners' experience.** No need to be humiliated in your first year of playing FF simply because you played with very experienced owners who know much more about the hobby due to years of experience. **Similarly, do not fall for the beginner trap of playing in a TD-only league.** Many beginners leagues use TDs as their only scoring mechanism. These leagues score only TDs (hence the name), but introduce way too much luck. They tend to be measures of luck, rather than skill, at predicting football.

There may be some overlap between skill level and some of the other variables mentioned in this chapter. For example, a beginner's league may limit the number of players on a roster or that can start. An experienced league has far less structured rules and allows owners to employ any strategy they choose. By selecting a beginner league, you may get more of the beginner tips mentioned in this chapter. **Smaller rosters favor beginners** because you have less players to draft and more players available to fix mistakes and team needs from free agency. **Small starter requirements also favor beginners** as it means less decisions.

Playoff Format

Your choice for determining the league champion is no playoffs, multi-week playoff or single championship game. If no playoffs are desired, then at the end of the regular season the team with the best winning percentage wins the league championship. One advantage to having no playoffs is that the regular season can be played through week 17. Another advantage of the no playoff system is that all of the teams in the league get to compete for the entire season. If you want just one championship game, do you want to use week 16 or 17? I suggest week 16 for reasons I will mention later. The two teams with the best record or the one with the best record and the highest scoring team could meet.

If you do want some type of elimination playoffs, you need to determine how many teams do you want in the postseason tournament. Playoffs can start as early as week 12 or as late as week 16. **The advantage of a playoff format is the excitement and intensity of single elimination. I recommend beginners play in a league with a playoff format and at least four teams in the playoffs**. The downside is that owners who do not make the playoffs have little to play for (having a bonus for high points each week helps create motivation for such teams).

Usually 12-team leagues go with four playoff teams and have playoffs in weeks 15 and 16 (if week 17 is used for the Super Bowl, then six teams can make the playoffs and the #1 and #2 seeds get byes in week 15). Having six teams in the playoffs usually means that two teams will get a bye in the first round of the playoffs and then will meet the two winners from round 1.

Most 14-team leagues use six teams making the playoffs in week 14 (#1 and #2 seeds get a bye) and the playoffs continue in week 15 with the Super Bowl in week 16.

Super Bowl Week 16 or 17

More leagues avoid week 17 than play in it. The problem with having the Super Bowl in week 17 is that many NFL teams who have clinched their playoff spot and have nothing to gain in week 17 will sit their stars on the bench or play them sparingly. This drives fantasy football fans nuts if they have their league Super Bowl in week 17 and their starting QB Peyton Manning is not playing or only plays the first quarter in order to avoid injury (this happened in 2009). **Better to avoid leagues with the FF Super Bowl scheduled during NFL week 17 because there are usually some players who do not play that week for this reason.** Yes, the same things can happen in week 16, but they are far less likely to occur and most coaches do not want their team to get too lackadaisical about their game performance. Of course, your choice of when to play your Super Bowl will also affect your playoffs and potentially how many regular season games you play.

Prizes

Look at how the league awards prizes. How much of the entry fee remains after administration costs, such as league management service, draft board and trophies? **A good ROT is first place gets 50%, second place gets 20% and third place gets their entry fee back.** Avoid leagues that award prizes to too many places. The object is to win!

I like leagues to have some prize money for weekly high scorers and the regular season high points team. Prizes are best when everyone has a chance to win something, even if they are not in a playoff hunt. A weekly prize for the highest scoring team works great for weeks 1-15. (Week 16 is the Super Bowl and thus the highest scoring team that week is going to win the big prize.)

Some argue that prizes should be all or nothing. In this case, the champion would get all the prize money. Again, these leagues breed apathy when an owner is out of contention. **The best format for beginners is to award prizes each week so that everyone has a chance to win something and stays competitive, and then award bigger prizes for the top three finishers only.**

Specialty Leagues

There are many variations of FF leagues. One specialty league is an Individual Defensive Player (IDP) league. Instead of drafting the entire defense of an NFL team, owners draft specific defensive players like the defensive tackle for the Dallas Cowboys or the linebacker for the Pittsburgh Steelers. Another variation is a keeper or dynasty league. In these leagues, owners can keep some or all (dynasty) of their players from the past season. **Both IDP and Keeper/Dynasty leagues are tougher for beginners and should be avoided until you have more experience**. See Chapter 13 for more on these types of leagues or _Fantasy Football Guidebook_ for a detailed explanation on both Keeper and IDP leagues.

There is one other type of league that may or may not be good for a beginner. This is the Points per Reception (PPR) league. In this format, players awarded a point (and sometimes more) for each pass they catch during a game. Different rules can be applied but, in general, each player receiving a pass is given one point for each catch. This is a great offensive position equalizer (strengthens WR/TE versus RB and QB), but can be harder to predict for the novice. **I am such a fan of these leagues and the parity they bring that I cannot find myself ruling them out for beginners.** However, do understand that a PPR rule benefits the experienced owner.

Number of Leagues

It goes without saying that the more leagues you play in, the more time you will need to spend on each. Therefore **I recommend a beginner start with just one league their first season.** See if you like it and how much time you want to put into it. If you have played one year and want to expand into another league in your second year - go for it. However, do not join 10 leagues in your first year. You will spread yourself too thin and you will not play some of your teams as competitively as if you had stuck to one league.

Summary

Checklist for picking a league:
1) Start with a free or low cost league
2) Play in a public league unless you know those in the private league
3) H2H is better for a beginner learning the nuances of the game
4) Make sure the draft is a traditional serpentine draft (not an auction)
5) Try to play in a league with 10 or 12 teams (the more teams there are, the harder it is to add good players later)
6) Avoid playing in a league with the Super Bowl in week 17
7) Start with a lower skill level league if possible (but avoid TD-only leagues)

8) Play in a league with playoffs and at least four teams that make the playoffs

9) Choose a league where the prizes are available every week and the top teams get the most

10) Avoid specialty leagues (IDP, Keeper, Dynasty, Auction, etc.) as a beginner

Chapter 4 How do the Rules affect me?

This chapter will provide a broad overview of some of the more popular FF rules. More detailed rules are covered in later chapters. Scoring, drafts, free agency and trades are just a few of the additional topics that will have rules governing them. Ultimately, you pick the rules you want to play by, simply by joining a league and thereby agreeing to abide by those rules.

The rules mentioned in this book, _Fantasy Football Basics_, are by no means the only version of FF. That is what makes this game/hobby so much fun. There is no right or wrong way to play it. There are no golden rules nor ancient royal society that decides what is official and what is not. You decide what league to play in and thus agree to the rules. You live by the rules, and you win or lose by the rules of the league(s) you choose to play in.

The rules, once set before the draft, should remain the same for the entire season. The worst thing that can happen is a rule change after the season has started, because that will affect owners after they have made decisions based on the former rules. Always check to see how easy it is for the rules to be changed. You do not want the rules to be changed until the end of the season.

Just like playing monopoly and buying the railroads and then finding out you cannot build hotels on them; you need to know the rules of your league so that you know what strategies can pay off. **Knowing your league's rules can be a big advantage.** It sounds easy and it is, but many owners do not know all the rules in the league. They may not realize all the ways a player can score or they may not know that rosters can be any number of players from any position. Knowing the rules inside and out (or knowing where to find them) can be an easy advantage.

Roster Size

The roster size is the total number of players/defenses on your fantasy team. In most leagues, the roster size is limited to an even number so that the draft can be an even number of rounds and thus not give any team an advantage (see Chapter 7 - Draft). This number determines how many rounds the draft will last. The larger the number of rounds, the longer the draft lasts and the bigger the fantasy team you manage.

The more players you own, the fewer players there will be available to choose from if you need to replace someone (and vice versa). This is also affected by how many teams are playing in the league. The more teams that play, the fewer players available after the draft.

In general, plan to have twice as many players (2x) as you need to start each week. So, if you have to start 10 players, plan on a total roster of 20 players. Obviously, some leagues have smaller rosters, and some have bigger rosters than the 2x rule above and this will affect the game's strategy (for more information about roster size strategy see *Fantasy Football Guidebook*).

Roster size will have some affect on who to draft and when. How many players to draft from each position will be determined by how many you start and how many extra players you have on your bench.

For beginners I recommend leagues with smaller rosters, that way you can seek replacements if needed and your draft day prep is less since there are fewer players to choose.

The number of players kept at each position will change based on where you are in the season and how strong (deep) you are at the position. For example, if the rules allow you to NOT draft a kicker in the initial draft, then skip that position if you can add a kicker before the season starts through free agency. Thus, you may not have a kicker until just before the season begins. Then in December, when the weather gets nasty and the free agency opportunities may be closed, you may want to carry two kickers (one as a backup). If you are strong at RB, you may elect not to have too many extra RBs and go for more WRs.

Lineup

Each owner is responsible for setting a weekly lineup (also known as the starting roster). The lineup requirement is stipulated in the rules and should be the same for the entire season. Lineups usually contain players from the offense who score points (TDs), or gain other measurable statistics like rushing, passing or receiving yards or catch passes (receptions). Therefore, most lineups include at least one QB, RB, WR, TE and K. Many leagues also add another RB and one or more WRs, since that is what every NFL team has as its starting formation. Read your league rules now and see what the starting lineup has to be.

Some leagues do not have TEs because the TE tends to have lesser stats compared to the WR. Still other leagues lump TEs in the same category as WR and ask owners to simply start two receivers, in which case, an owner can start two WRs, two TEs or one of each.

Some leagues have one or more positions that can be a RB, WR or a TE. This is known as a "flex" position. It gives the owner the flexibility to start a RB, WR or TE, depending on whom he thinks will score more points that week.

Numerous leagues will also add some component to account for defenses. In many leagues, this is the entire defense from an NFL team. Therefore, in addition to the individual offensive players drafted, you may also have a defense or two on your roster. In many cases this defense (DEF) also includes a special teams (ST) component. Check your league rules carefully to see if the defense includes the special teams. ST involve kickoff and punt returns and score on TDs on those returns.

Realize that changing the number of starters can also affect the relative value of that position. Some leagues require that only one RB start, which decreases demand and thus increases supply. Still other leagues combine the WR and TE positions, thus reducing the need for all but the best TEs. Some leagues require that three WRs start, thus increasing demand for that position and increasing the relative value of a WR.

Many leagues have a starting lineup of one QB, two RBs, two-three WRs, one TE, one K and one DEF/ST. You can expect to start nine to ten players. Leagues with flex players are more difficult. **If possible, stick to a league without a flex as a beginner.**

Free Agency (FA) Rules

Free agency is the process of adding different players to your team after the initial draft. This "need" may arise because of injury, suspension, retirement, poor play or a logistical need due to bye weeks that overlap. There are at least six different FA methods that a league may use.

6 ways of Dealing with FA/Waiver Wire

1) First come, first served (FCFS)

Literally, the first owner to ask for a player gets him. This benefits those who are watching all ten hours of football live on Sunday when the injuries occur. I have been in leagues where the backup who just entered the huddle is picked up, while the starter lies on a stretcher on the field. That is the Sunday NFL Ticket and wireless internet for you. FCFS allows adds/drops at any time. It is a disadvantage to those of us who have to do things on Sunday like cut the grass, or go to a child's recital. **Avoid leagues that are FCFS** since beginners will not benefit as much.

2) Weekly FA

This is awarded based on rankings (also known as worst to first format). All adds/drops occur at a set time in the week, usually Wednesday. At this time, any player who has been claimed by more than one team is awarded to the team with the worst record. As a tiebreaker, the player would go to the team with the lowest total FPs scored to date for the current season. The waiver wire ranking is adjusted each week based on record. Advantage: All owners have a chance to get a player who is suddenly now a starter. Thus, it does not reward the 24/7 football addict, it instead helps to promote parity in the league. Disadvantage: It rewards owners who drafted poorly or who do not manage their team well. Thus, the 0-6 goofus has a great RB fall in his lap through no skill of his own. It also prevents teams from adding replacements right up until game time*, based on injuries and other game time developments and penalizes winning teams.

3) Waiver wire system

Same as #2 above, but the waiver priority starts out based on where you drafted, and once you claim a player you go to the bottom of the priority list. Thus, if you have the last pick in a 10-team draft, you would have the #1 priority for the first claim you made. However, once you make a claim, you then fall to #10 on the waiver wire priority list. Advantage: Rewards owners who got worst picks in draft, does not reward bad drafters or bad managers of their teams. Disadvantages: Still does not allow replacement player additions up until game time*.

4) Blind bidding

Each team starts with 1,000 free agent "dollars" in their free agent aquistion budget (FAAB) for the season. Teams bid on players weekly. No team knows the other's bids until the winning bids have been awarded. The team with the highest bid is awarded that player. The winning team's FAAB is reduced by the winning bid amount and a player must be dropped to make room for the new acquisition. Once a team's FAAB reaches zero, they cannot bid on players. Advantages: Fairest system. Disadvantages: Hard to run on your own, no game day injuries plan*.

5) No transactions at any time

These leagues do not allow FA pickups, but instead have a supplemental draft. In most cases teams must have larger rosters and bench spots to allow for injuries, suspensions, etc.; otherwise owners will find themselves and their teams so far behind by the time the supplemental FA draft comes around that it will do them no good.

6) Limit the number of transactions

This can be a weekly limit (the most common limit is two transactions per week) or a seasonal limit. Trades and FA pickups count toward the transactions. In rare cases, moving a player from starter to the bench (and vice versa) will count.

Some leagues have a transactions deadline for the season. After this time, no adds/drops or trades can be performed.

*One way to avoid the disadvantage of not allowing add/drop until game time is to make the above processes only applicable from first kickoff until the mid-week deadline. After the Wednesday deadline, when players have been claimed, the process turns into a FCFS process until the first game starts. Once the first game starts the process of claiming, a player is frozen until the next week's deadline on Wednesday. This prevents an owner from gaining an advantage by watching football games where an injury occurs.

Trades

Some leagues use a trading deadline to prevent collusion. However, if used, the deadline must be early enough to stop teams that are out of contention from dumping, but late enough to allow teams to navigate the bye weeks. Week 11 seems like a great choice.

Some leagues rely on the commissioner's approval of trades; others rely on owners to vote to approve trades or veto trades (certain number vetoing = trade not put through); other leagues have an early trading deadline to prevent collusion for a playoff push. **Avoid leagues with trades, if possible.** If playing in a league that allows trades, try to keep the commissioner out of the business of approving trades. Make it an owners vote (See Chapter Eleven – Trades for a detailed explanation of trades).

Summary

1) Know the rules of your league (and how to take advantage of them).
2) A league with smaller rosters is better for beginners because it requires less draft preparation (you draft fewer total players so your rankings do not have to be as comprehensive).
3) Leagues with smaller rosters also mean a more abundant supply of free agents to choose from, thus making a replacement choice easier.
4) Avoid leagues that use FCFS free agency during the early part of the week.
5) Avoid the harder lineup decisions involved with flex positions.

Chapter 5 What are the Scoring Rules?

The players on your FF team score points by scoring in the NFL (thru TDs, FGs, etc.) or accumulating yardage. If you elect to start them, their statistics count towards your fantasy team's weekly score. If the player is on your bench (you did not elect to start him for the week) then the points do NOT count toward your team's weekly score. The number of points they get for each action are determined by the league's scoring system.

Often what sets a league apart from another league is the scoring system it implements. For some leagues this has been a lifelong pursuit, with growing pains and yearly tweaking to get it exactly right for the owners. Other leagues picked a system early on and have never changed it. **The bottom line is that you want the league to be fun and if it is not fun because of the scoring system, do not play in it.** The NFL tracks, and makes available to the public, endless categories of statistics from each week's games. This opens up limitless possibilities for scoring rules. No rule is wrong, some are just better than others are for certain leagues and certain owners.

Before I get into the nuances of scoring systems, I want to start with one basic difference between FF leagues. In most instances, rushing and receiving TDs are awarded six points. Passing TDs however, are usually only awarded three or four points, since there are generally many more TD passes than TD runs. In 2009, Drew Brees (QB, New Orlean Saints) led the league with 34 passing TDs. Adrian Peterson (RB, MIN) led with just 17 rushing TDs. If QBs were awarded six points for every TD pass thrown, then that position would become much more valuable than the other positions (based on the 33-50% more points QBs would get). Another argument against awarding six points for passing TDs is that it takes away the advantage of a rushing QB. If you awarded all TDs six points, then the rushing QBs Donovan McNabb (QB, Washington Redskins) and Aaron Rodgers (QB, Green Bay Packers) would be under-valued when compared to the Drew Brees and Peyton Mannings (QB, Indianapolis Colts) of the world.

Note: Some leagues do award six points for all TDs, so beware! Check your rules now and if QBs get six points for passing TDs, remember to rank them higher overall.

Therefore, the first scoring difference between leagues is how many points they assign to a passing TD. This will have a huge impact on your draft order (QBs will be worth more, and thus drafted earlier, if awarded six points instead of three or four points).

Each year the number of different scoring systems in use by FF leagues increases. Most will fall into the following broad categories: Basic, Performance, Bonus or Distance.

Basic Scoring

In basic leagues (also sometimes called TD-only leagues), the scoring is an attempt to mirror the NFL as closely as possible. In most instances, rushing and receiving TDs are worth six points. Passing TDs, however, are usually only awarded three or four points. Two-point conversions can either be worth two points for each individual involved in carrying out a successful two-point conversion pass (i.e. P. Manning (QB, IND) gets two points, as does Reggie Wayne (WR, IND) who caught the pass) or, as owners in some leagues believe, because only two points were scored only two should be awarded. In this scenario, Peyton and Reggie would each receive one point. Players sucessfully rushing two-point conversions are awarded the full two points.

Kickers get three points for every FG they kick and one point for every successful extra point. In keeping with the basic principle of being "just like the NFL," defenses are awarded two points for safeties and six points for any TD scored by the defense or the special teams unit (i.e. a kickoff or punt returned for a TD).

One example of a basic scoring system is:

Rush TD	= 6
Receiving TD	= 6
Pass TD	= 4
Two-point conversion rush	= 2
Two-point conversion pass	= 1 for passer and receiver
FG	= 3
XP	= 1
Safety	= 2
DEF TD	= 6
KO/PR TD	= 6

The basic system is easier to keep track of by individual owners on a Sunday afternoon because it only involves scoring TDs by their players. The owners can keep track of every team's scoring with just a pencil and a piece of paper. The downside to this is that the scoring tends to be a little haphazard. Your RB can rush for 200 yards but be taken out for some rest and the fullback (or third down back) comes in and scores three TDs. You end up with zero points while the "TD" back (think Willis McGahee) scores all the points. It is very frustrating to see your starting RB bust one loose and run 85 yards only to be tackled at the 2-yard line and then come out for some much-needed oxygen, as someone else gets the TD rush. **TD-only leagues are more about luck and less about proving who the best owner is, therefore avoid TD-only scoring leagues, not only for beginners but all FF players.**

In the examples shown in this chapter, all individuals can score points for the actions. The player does not have to be a QB to get points for throwing a TD pass, or have to be a WR/TE to get points for catching a TD pass. LaDainian Tomlinson (LT) has caught, thrown and rushed for a TD in a single game. He would get six points for the TD catch, four for the TD pass and six for the TD rush, for a total of 16 points in the basic format above. Check your leagues rules though, as some leagues only allow scoring to come from the position that normally does the task (i.e only RBs score for rushing TDs and only QBs can score for passing TDs). **If this is the case, some QBs and RBs will need to be downgraded in your rankings.**

The FFPC has action scoring. In action scoring, any TD scored by a player counts as a TD for fantasy scoring purposes. Kickoff and punt return TDs are awarded to the player who scored them in the FFPC. Even if it is a defensive TD like the one Marques Colsten (WR, New Orlean Saints) had in 2009; it would count in the FFPC, but not in most leagues.

Performance Scoring (sometimes called yardage scoring)

Performance scoring involves the basic format but adds points for yardage. The most common method is to award one point for every 10 rushing/receiving yards. The passers also get one point for every 20 yards passing (sometimes this is per 25 yards, if 20 yards is too much of an advantage). Therefore, if your RB runs for 200 yards but has no TDs in a game; he still ends up with 20 points (200/10 = 20). Some leagues use decimals (i.e. points less than one) and some only use whole numbers in their calculations (so 19 yards is either 1.9 points or 1 point). The advantage of yardage scoring is that it makes the games more fun to watch, because now every play means something for your players. In the basic league, if you are watching your RB and he is backed up in his own red zone, each rush is not significant unless he breaks one for a TD or they drive down to the opponent's red zone. In yardage leagues, every rush from scrimmage can offer the possibility of points. Three 4-yard rushes now give you 1 or 1.2 points, depending on the format for that league.

Kickers get involved too, because in many leagues yardage scoring for kickers means getting points for how long a FG was. Any FG inside 30 yards is three points; any outside 30 is worth the distance divided by 10. Therefore, a 48-yard FG is worth 4.8 points, or 4 points if dropping decimals. The defense had to have a performance statistic, so they are awarded based on how many points they allow their opponent to score (or, less often, how many offensive yards they give up in a game). In many formats a shutout equals 10 points and holding your opponent's score to under seven is worth five points and fewer than 14 is worth three points.

I recommend that you play in leagues with performance scoring (and PPR mentioned later) since these leagues remove more of the "luck" factor.

The most common performance scoring method is:

Every 10 yards rushing/receiving	= 1 Point
Every 25 yards passing	= 1 Point
Rushing/receiving TD	= 6 Points
Passing TD	= 3 or 4 Pts
Interceptions	= -1 Point
FG	= yardage/10 (min. 3 points)
Extra points	= 1 Point
Defense/ST sacks and turnovers	= 1 Point
Safeties	= 2 Points
Defensive TDs	= 6 Points
DEF	= 10 points for allowing no points to opponents; 5 points if score is 6 or less; 3 points if the score is under 14

Bonus Scoring (also known as milestone scoring)

Bonus scoring developed for those who liked the idea of spicing up the basic format, but were afraid of getting too complicated and taking the game out of the hands of the owners and putting it on a computer with advanced mathematics to tally the score. The result was bonus scoring or milestone scoring. In this format, players are awarded bonus points for exceeding a set amount of yardage in rushing, receiving and passing. The most common bonus points are for 100 yards rushing or receiving and 300 yards passing. These achievements are easy to track during Sunday's games. CBS has a great ticker at the bottom of the screen to show game scores and individual stats for QB/RB/WR/K/Def. It was initiated for the fantasy football fan.

> Passing 300 or more yards = 3 bonus points (1 point for every 50 yards after 300)
>
> Rushing 100 yards or more = 3 bonus points (2 points for every 50 yards after 100)
>
> Receiving 100 yards or more = 3 bonus points (2 points for every 50 yards after 100)
>
> Kicking a FG of 50 or more yards = 2 bonus points (on top of the 3 awarded for every FG)
>
> Defenses would get a bonus for shutouts = 10 points

Avoid Bonus scoring systems too because they suffer the same problems as the basic scoring system. Players who are just shy of the bonus yardage get no credit for their achievements.

Distance Scoring

Distance scoring takes the basics of performance scoring and adds points for the distance of the TD play. This "premium" only applies to plays that score TDs. Generally, any TD play of more than 40 yards will get a bonus of 2 points. In distance scoring, if Larry Johnson rushes twice in a game for two TDs; one of 65 yards and the other 34 yards, then he would get 6 points for each TD rush and 2 points for the distance TD over 40 yards. He would also get 9.9 points for his total rushing yards of 99. This would mean a FP total of 6+6+2+9.9 = 23.9. Some leagues award more points the longer the TD play. For example, a TD rush that is over 80 yards may be worth 6 additional points! This is also sometimes called the "big play league" since TDs are worth more the longer they are. Some QBs and WRs can be "big play" performers and the offensive scheme they play in can be an indicator. (Tom Brady and Randy Moss come to mind.)

In this format, FGs are also rewarded based on longer distances. FGs inside 39 yards are worth 3 points; over 40 yards are the distance divided by 10. A 45-yard FG would be worth 4.5 points. A field goal from anywhere between 40-49 yards is worth 4 points in leagues without decimals and 50 or greater yard FGs are valued at 5 points.

Avoid Distance scoring leagues since they introduce more luck than skill in predicting player performance. Often the difference between a 5 yard gain and an 80 yard TD is a missed tackle or blown coverage. It does not show any additional skill for the offensive player and is more likely to occur due to a lucky break.

Miscellaneous Scoring Rules

Points per Reception (PPR): This method typically awards 1 point for any reception made by an individual player. This is called the great equalizer. In many leagues the RB is more powerful because he scores more TDs than the WRs and TEs. But PPR gives the WR and TE more value and a better chance to score fantasy points. This is especially helpful in leagues that require a TE on the starting roster. TEs will rarely score and do not usually rack up huge yardage or distance numbers, but they will make many catches and this equalizes that position among QBs and RBs. Don't count all the RBs out of this category. Many RBs also catch the ball out of the backfield, like Steven Jackson and Matt Forte. For this reason, some leagues (NFFC) only award .5 points for a RB reception. The FFPC goes to the other extreme for TEs. They award 1.5 points per TE catch.

What happens if you give 1 point per reception? The WR and TE will get the biggest boost, then the RB. The QB will get no boost and thus drop further down the food chain (overall rankings). What you will find is that QBs, RBs and WRs will all be much closer in the number of points scored. PPR definitely helps the top 10 TEs. The TEs who catch more than 40 passes a year are more valuable than before. The decline in the position after TE10 is still pronounced, thus making it a priority to grab a TE early in the draft.

I have written it before but will repeatit again (it is that important). **Know the rules of your league**. It can be a big advantage. Are QBs penalized for interceptions? If yes, how much? There is a big difference between zero points, minus one point and minus two points for an interception. Are defenses awarded 10 points for a shutout? If yes, and they play STL, DET or CLE, they may score a shutout this season. Are kickers penalized for missed FGs or XPs? If yes, which kicker has the best accuracy? If not, who cares?

Summary

1) Make sure the league's scoring rules are fun. If they are too cumbersome, and you cannot understand how they are determined, avoid the league.
2) Determine how passing TDs are scored. Most give 3 to 4 points. If a league awards 6 points, rank the QBs higher overall.
3) Avoid leagues that base their scoring on TDs only, bonus points or distance of TDs. Each of these types of scoring systems places too much emphasis on luck.
4) Play in a league that uses the performance system for scoring (TDs, yardage and points per catch).
5) Make sure players score on all TDs, not just some.

Chapter 6 How do I Rank Players (positions)?

You need to identify the players who will score the most FPs. Later, Chapter 8 discusses ranking individual players by positions for a cheat sheet. This chapter will discuss player positions in general terms, so that you can understand the trends at each position. Finally, some common terms used in evaluating players are explained.

Think of your fantasy football team as an army. You need a general to lead (QB), infantry to slog it out on the ground (RBs), an air force to bomb deep (WRs), marines to fight the tough battles (TE), artillery to hit the enemy (K) and special forces to take the attack to the enemy behind their lines (DEF/ST). You only need one good general (QB), but you need lots of infantry (RBs) and aircraft (WRs).

Quarterback

QBs are the generals of the playing field. **A common beginner mistake is to draft a QB early (1st or 2nd round) simply because they are the big names of football.** Who can resist having a Peyton Manning or Tom Brady on their team? The name recognition alone gives these Top QBs value in the bragging department. However, as an owner you need to weigh potential production, not fame appeal, when deciding who to draft with your top pick on draft day.

Things to watch: Who is he throwing it to? Good WRs make QBs great. How is the offensive line? What is his defense like (will he get the ball back a lot)?

QBs tend to bloom at 26 or 27 years old, which is about four or five years into their career; about the time when they stop rushing so much and stay in the pocket. Stay away from rookies and even second year QBs, who generally do not fair too well.

I recommend two possible strategies for beginners. Draft either the fourth or the fifth Top QB, or wait until the next to last team has their QB and then get your QB last. If you want to get a Top QB, wait until the third QB is drafted, then grab either the fourth or the fifth QB with your next pick if he is available. The fourth or fifth drafted QB has a good chance to finish 2nd or 3rd at the end of the season. If there is a run on QBs and you cannot get one of the Top 5 with your next pick, then fall back and wait on QB and get one of the last of the mid-round 11th -13th QBs.

Most of the top QBs are not worth the high draft spot you pay for them, because most QBs tend to produce simular fantasy points. Sure, the top 2 or 3 are well above the pack, but the 4th QB and 10th QB were seperated by only 30 points in 2009. There is a large drop off after the 15th -18th QB.

You can wait on drafting a QB and still get one as good (if not better) than the one you passed on (Wait until the 8'th or 9'th round.) Waiting till everyone else has their QB, then grabbing both of yours, QB12 and QB13, costs you 14% of the top QB FP, but only a few points more than QB5+QB19. If you are going to draft a Top 5 QB, great, but the next best strategy is to wait and get the '10th to 12th best and pair them up with another QB thereafter.

If you decide to go QB12, then go QB13 next. The beauty of this strategy is you get better RBs and WRs (critical positions) and chances are one of the QBs (12th or 13th QB) will be a Top 8 QB anyway. Worst-case scenario - both are in the middle of the rankings, but you can start the one with the best matchup each week to get the same amount of points as a Top 8 QB.

Injury affects this position to some degree, although QBs are not as injury prone as they were a few years ago. The NFL has dedicated rules to protecting the QBs and few are injured as much. Most QBs miss a game during the year (Peyton Manning and Brett Favre are exceptions to this rule). So draft a QB and expect him to start every game, except his bye week.

Running Back

RBs are the infantry, or bulk, of your fantasy team. A good fantasy team has to have reliable, high scoring RBs. You can be weak in other areas (TE, K or DEF), but a strong RB corps is a must. In fact, in some leagues, a great RB (think LaDainian Tomlinson (RB, SD) in 2005 or 2006 or Chris Johnson in 2009) can carry a fantasy team into the playoffs and to a championship.

RBs are influenced by supply and demand (see appendix A Supply and Demand Table). There are only 32 NFL teams and most have one main RB. Some teams have running back by committee (RBBC), where two or more RBs share the workload (estimated at 14 teams in 2010). This can create problems for fantasy owners because it is hard to determine which RB will get the most FPs each week. It is much simpler if you have a clear starting RB on your fantasy team. However, if each fantasy team starts 2 RBs and everyone wants a backup RB too, that is 36 RBs desired (2+1 x 12 teams=36) and only 46 in supply (18 teams with 1 RB and 14 teams with 2 RBs in RBBC). If an injury occurs to one team, they will be without a RB unless they have drafted his backup. The backup RB is a handcuff (HC) since you are drafting both RBs. **Get your stud RB's HC (backup).** This way you have insurance in case your #1 RB is injured.

The RB is your franchise. It is the most important position in fantasy football. They score a ton of TDs. RBs will score from 10-20 TDs, whereas WRs score 8-12 and TEs 5-10 TDs. There is good reason for the old saying: "RBs early and often." Due to their scarcity, it is better to have too many rather than too few at RB.

Watch to see if he is an every down running back or just plays on 1st and 2nd downs. Does he get the goal line carries or does he have some vulture waiting to snatch those TDs from him? **Does he catch balls well out of the backfield (Like Matt Forte or Steven Jackson - important in a PPR league)?** Is he stable on and off the field? Does he have a good potent offense (Indianapolis, New Orleans) or does the team always find itself behind at halftime (Detroit Lions, Houston Texans)? What is his defense like? Watch out for a poor QB. Bad QBs can hurt a RBs performance since he will not be on the field as much if the QB cannot move the ball down the field. Both Steven Jackson and DeAngelo Williams suffered because of poor QB play in 2009.

Do not be too afraid of a rookie RB because they can learn their position more quickly than any other scoring position in the NFL. Do, however, watch the inevitable rookie hype (hint: overpriced). Many rookie RBs will be talked about in the media, but few live up to 1st year expectations.

Historically, less than 50% of the top 3 RBs have repeated in the next year. Why? RBs are notorious for injuries and the NFL has such parity, thanks to free agency, that a good team last year could be a mediocre team this year. Do not get upset if you have a late first round draft spot. You can nail it by getting the correct pick of who is left. And where will this year's Top 3 RB come from? There is a good chance it will be RBs ranked 5-15 last year.

Avoid RBs over 30, as most RBs who make it to their 10'th year do not do as well. (Tiki Barber and John Riggins are the exceptions). RBs can be power-oriented (run-you-over type backs like Clinton Portis) or cutback runners (Kevin Faulk). Big RBs that do not share time can be traded early, before they are dinged up, as they will start to falter in the second half of the season. Big RBs who share time should be saved for the stretch run, as they tend to do better in the second half. RBs that are involved in the passing game tend to do as well, if not better, in the second half of the season. Rookie RBs tend to outperform in the second half of the season as well.

1) RBs need two things; talent and opportunity. Opportunity comes from having a good OL and playing time.

2) Youth is everything to a RB. One of the three top-drafted rookie RBs will break out. Most will break out in their 2nd – 4th year, depending on opportunity. **The first RB drafted in the NFL draft is a stud 80% of the time.** The percentages drop dramatically after that.

Wide Receiver

WRs are the "Air Force" of your fantasy team. They can strike deep behind enemy lines and deliver a devastating knock out punch with a long bomb pass. There are lots of WRs. Each team has at least 3 WRs who will start for differing amounts of playing time. Even though WRs are abundant (3 WRs x 32 NFL teams= 96 Starting WRs), finding the top WRs can be difficult.

They are the second most important position behind RBs. They too are affected by supply and demand (see Appendix A) because some leagues start 3 WRs or add a flex that can be a WR. This puts pressure to get good WRs. If a league starts 3 WRs, and if you allow for byes, that means you need 4 per team at a minimum, which is 48 in a 12-team league (See Appendix D). There are 64 WR1 and WR2s but the quality goes downhill after about WR30.

What kind of WR? There are two types of WRs, speed and possession. Possession receivers do not have the speed to get open deep but are surer-handed. They are the ones crossing the middle of the field, getting many receptions and some yardage but not as many TDs. Generally the older a receiver is, the more he becomes a possession receiver and must learn to find the seams in a defense and "sit down" in a scheme to catch the underneath balls. The speed (or long ball or TD) WR will stretch the field and go deep more often, thus he will have more TDs and longer yardage TDs. They will generally be the younger WRs.

Usually it takes 2-3 years in the NFL for players to get comfortable at this position and one year to learn a new team's system. **WRs tend to break out in their 2nd or 3rd year. WRs tend to drop out of the Top 10 in their 7th or 8th year.** They are generally not as tall as TEs, but recently tall WRs have become stars. **Great WRs need great QBs. Watch who is throwing to the WRs, it influences their production tremendously.**

Tight End

TEs are like the Marines: tough, determined and can go anywhere and do anything. Sometimes TEs are asked to stay behind and protect the QB (block); other times they are sent across the middle of the fiield. On these crossing routes, they need to make the tough catch near many defenders with a high probability of a painful tackle. In some instances, they are sent into the end zone and asked to leap high into the air to catch a pass only they can reach. TEs are hard to figure out.

Use the same criteria as WR for rankings. TEs need the same time to learn systems. Draft a Top 10 TE, after that, wait. The top 4-5 ranked TEs perform consistently and prove more valuable. These are the studs at TE, expect them to go in the 3rd-5th rounds. In past years, only a few TEs performed well enough to be worth a pick in rounds 3-5. **Now there are as many as 10 TEs that perform well enough to be drafted in rounds 4-8.** If your league does not have PPR and/or require a TE, then avoid all but the Top

5 TEs. If you have PPR and need a TE, then you need to expand your TE coverage (excuse the pun).

Kicker

Kickers are the artillery of your army. They can be powerful offensive weapons, unfortunately sometimes you do not know when or where they will have a great game. Kicker's performances vary from game to game, but over a season most score about the same. They are the only offensive player that is not guaranteed to play at least one play during a game (sometimes a kicker may not get a chance to kick a FG or XP depending on the offensive production). A kicker may have zero points one game and 15 points the next. Many kickers score about the same every year, yet the kickers who make the Top 5 fluctuate so much from year to year. This position is perhaps the hardest to predict in terms of fantasy point production. Because of that unpredictability, it is the least appreciated position (for good reason) and thus drafted last in many cases.

If you only have to draft one kicker, draft him in the next to last round. If you can avoid drafting a kicker all together, then do not draft a kicker. However, if you are forced to draft one (many leagues require you to draft a starting lineup), get him with the next to last pick of your draft. It is close enough to the end that you are not paying too high a price for him and it is not the last round (typical advice is to get a kicker in the last round) so you may have a better chance at a K in your top 5 list.

Last year the difference between the 3rd and 11th kicker was 18 points. That is a little over 1 point a game between one of the top kickers and one of the last kickers drafted. Rarely do Top 5 kickers repeat. You are better off looking for kickers that finished 10th-15th and have a good reason to do better. However, avoid kickers from poor scoring teams from the previous year. Teams generally do not improve or degrade rapidly from year to year. So, one of the bottom five scoring teams from last year is much more likely to be near the bottom this year. Again, do not panic if your kicker turns out to be a poor choice. There will be over half of the remaining kickers on the waiver wire to choose from for a replacement.

Favor kickers in domes or from teams with stadiums in favorable weather conditions (Florida and California teams) especially late in the season.

Defense/Special Team (DEF/ST)

Many leagues have defensive/special teams (DEF/ST also seen as DT/ST or D/ST) as one of their starting positions. In these cases, you draft the entire defense and special team of one NFL team. This is called a team defense. Whenever that team plays, your DEF/ST plays. For example, if you have Baltimore's defense then whenever Baltimore plays a game you would get any defensive/special team statistics from Baltimore. If they have three sacks, an interception and hold their opponents to zero points (a shutout), then you would get fantasy points for those events based on your league scoring.

The defense/special teams are the special forces of your army. The defense's job is to go behind enemy lines and get the ball back to their offense. Defenses can be two main types: tough and aggressive or bend but don't break. Baltimore is a tough, aggressive defense. They are proactive with lots of blitzes. New England is of the latter type, allowing opposing offenses to move the ball but knowing that an eventual breakdown will occur. ST help by pushing the offense further along by giving them better field position.

Defenses are a little better than kickers when it comes to FPs but not much. Defensive scoring depends so much on the offense they are playing, the weather and the field conditions. Defenses usually break out FPs-wise as the Top 3 and then 4th -8th and finally 9th-20th are pretty much the same points over the season. Only 16 points seperated DEF9 and DEF20 in 2009.

Defenses tend to remain the same from year to year. A good defense will, in all likelihood, stay good and vice versa the next year, barring a critical injury or the retirement of a key defensive player. So if they were good last year, by all means use that as an indicator for this year. Sacks are a good indicator too. The more times you hit the opposing QB, the more likely you are to intercept him or force a fumble, both of which can lead to defensive TDs.

Team defenses are an easy position to manage because with team defenses you do not have to worry about demotions, suspensions or injuries making your defense unavailable for play. The defense will always play (except on its bye week). Demotions, suspensions and injuries will affect how the team defense plays and these situations should be considered, but, in general, a team defense is an easy play, week in and week out.

Strategy: One easy technique is to pick one defense and let them play throughout the season based on the assumption that most defenses are the same statistically and if you play them every week (except for their bye week) then their scoring should average out. Look for a good defense that has a late bye week and play them until their bye week before analyzing the defense's scoring trends. If you do decide to draft just one defense, it could free up another roster spot (the other spot that a DEF/ST2 may have held) for a sleeper pick. Also be aware of the league rules, as you may have to pick a permanent defense or two before any free agency deadline for the season.

Another harder strategy to implement is to pick up two defenses in later rounds and alternate them based on their matchups, hoping to optimize their fantasy points This is called "defense by committee (DBC)." The theory behind DBC is that you can save a draft pick early on (i.e. not drafting one of the top 5 DEF/ST) and instead grab a couple of average defenses in later rounds, because the two average defenses have great matchups on different weeks that will provide the same fantasy points as the better defense drafted much earlier. It does not make sense to draft a top defense and use this method to draft a middle-of-the-road defense. You will be drafting both defenses earlier than you need. The objective is to find two middle-of-the road DEF/STs (based on your rankings) that will compliment each other when one faces a touch offense or is on a bye week. Things to look for: easy combined schedule based on last year's opponents and some tweaking of last year's offense based on this years expectations for those offenses, and defenses not in the top 10 ranking (so other owners do not grab one early, thus ruining your strategy). Note: You should not go into the draft expecting to get exactly these two defenses, instead have several committee pairs of defenses and go with whichever pair is still on the board when it is your time to draft a defense. For example, if your pairs are MIA+NE, MIN+DET and IND+SF, but NE has already been drafted and you suspect that a home town owner (called a Homer) will grab MIN next round, then take IND with your pick and grab SF before they should be drafted, according to your overall rankings. It may not have been your first choice for a defense pair but it is still a pair that will work in the DBC approach. Even better is to have IND and several other choices to choose from to matchup with their defense.

So far we have not mentioned special teams much. The special teams are the kickoff and punt return teams. If your DEF/ST scores a TD on a kickoff or punt return, then they are awarded those points. The Cleveland Browns special teams, with Josh Cribbs, provide some extra points when he runs a KR/PR for a TD. Generally, you do not want to pick a defense solely for its KR/PR record, nor do you want to pick a defense only for its defense. Look at both aspects when analyzing this position. **Do not forget about the Special Teams (ST) if they are included as part of the defense**. Know the rules! Most teams get 1 TD from a kickoff or punt return a year (not significant), but other teams like MIN, CLE or CHI have playmakers that can provide more TDs (FP standings changer).

If you plan on drafting just one defense (not a Top 3 DEF), draft a defense with your second to last pick (the pick before you draft a kicker). In many cases you can get a defense that is in the Top 8 on your rankings simply because after the consensus Top 3 defenses, many of the others are ranked all over the place. By waiting, you can secure a good enough defense without sacrificing too much in the early or mid-rounds of the draft. Note: This is if your league scores defenses primarily on turnovers and TDs. If points are awarded for yardage or points scored against the defense, consider moving your drafting of a defense up one or two spots.

Risky/Breakdown Players

Breakdown players are players who are past their prime and have a greater chance of injury or benching due to poor performance. I used to speculate on QBs, but Brett Favre and Kurt Warner proved me wrong for so many years that all QB analysis based on age is now out the window. However, studies show that **RB 30 years or older are more likely to breakdown. For WR, 34 seems to be the average age where WRs start to lose production**. (Jerry Rice is one well-known exception to this rule.)

Who is a Stud?

Your top 3-4 draft picks are your studs (your 4 best players). All players who are ranked in the top 10 at RB and WR are studs, as are the Top 5 QBs and TEs. You may even get a stud with your 4th draft pick, if drafting from the back end of the draft (picks 8-12). Why do you care who is a stud? **Never bench a stud unless he is hurt or benched (see Rule #3 Chapter 9)**

Who is a Sleeper?

A sleeper is someone who is relatively unknown and who performs much better than expected, based on his draft position. Think of them as something that may prove valuable that no one else may know about. You want to get them, but not too early and sacrifice a known player who could help your team. Sleepers give you a chance to break away from the other teams if they perform well. This sets you apart and gives you a better chance of winning a championship. I do not know how many times I have seen an owner draft well but never gamble on a sleeper or two. This owner only makes the playoffs half of the time and never understands why I always make the playoffs. It is because I take a few chances, and when they payout it means I have a great player that no one expected. The sleeper who hits (performs well) gives me the extra edge I need to make the playoffs. The trick is finding the sleepers.

The key is to have at least five sleeper picks ranked in order of expected draft position (i.e. which round you think other owners will draft them if given the chance). That way when someone steals a sleeper or two it will not destroy your whole sleeper plan. Having just two or three sleepers and seeing them taken before you can pull the trigger is a bit demoralizing. Of course, the later the round you take a sleeper, the more the payoff if he performs (because hopefully you picked someone with value ahead of him, rather than grabbing your sleeper a round earlier).

Tips for Picking Sleepers

1) Look for a window of opportunity. Remember Skill+Opportunity = Success. Does the starter have injury problems, contractual issues, off-the-field problems, fumbling problems? Is there a new coach or system to get used to? Did the team add/lose another player (add stud RB/ lose WR#1) who can help?

2) More sleepers are of the young variety than the old variety. **Look at 2nd or 3rd year players** simply because they have had time to learn their systems and make the rookie mistakes. **You are more likely to find a sleeper in someone who has not been in the league more than four or five years.** If they have been playing longer, then they have had their chance and it probably has passed them by. There are exceptions to this, but for the most part go with youth for sleepers.

WR Sleepers

WRs make the best candidates for sleepers so look for:

1) Look for WRs in their 2nd-5th year (who are 1st round NFL picks) who had 40+ receptions, 2+ TDs, 400+ yards and that are the starters (WR1 or WR2) on their team. They should have a consistent QB throwing to them and be completely free of injury.

2) Rookie WRs rarely (5% of the time) breakout. A breakout season occurs when a player greatly exceeds expectations. Rookies who do well in their first year (50+ receptions and 700+ yards) tend to breakout the next year.

3) Look for dedication to the craft. Look for the WRs who arrive early and stay late; the ones who practice in the off-season with their QB or take extra time before every game to practice with their QB (Reggie Wayne). These are the ones who will provide consistent performance because it is hard to catch a pigskin thrown from a human being unless you practice it.

Read *Fantasy Football Tips* for more information on how to find sleepers.

Draft Steals and Busts

What is a "steal" in the draft; any player drafted two or more rounds below where he finished in the end of season rankings based on total fantasy points. If I drafted a WR in the 5th round with the 53rd pick (5.05) and he finishes 24 places higher or more, then he was a steal (29th overall in points scored; 3rd round, 5th pick).

A player who performs one round better than where he was picked would be considered a good pick. Again, in a 12-team league that would be a player who finishes 12 spots higher in the rankings than his pick.

An early (reach) pick would be a player who finishes a round further down the rankings.

A bust would be a player who finishes more than two rounds lower than he was drafted.

These are terms owners use to describe potential players in the draft.

Summary

1) Draft a Top 5 QB (preferbaly the 4th or 5th QB drafted) or wait and get the 10th or 11th QB.
2) Beginners fall in love with QBs and draft them too early (1st or 2nd round).
3) RBs need talent and opportunity. Look for both.
4) The first rookie RB drafted in the NFL draft is a stud 80% of the time.
5) Look for WRs in their 2nd or 3rd year as sleepers and avoid WRs after 8 years of NFL service.
6) Great WRs need great QBs.
7) Wait on TEs. Target a Top 10 TE in rounds 4-8.
8) Draft your kicker in the next to last round.
9) Draft your defense one round before the kicker.
10) Do not forget ST with DEF, if rules allow.
11) Beware RBs over 30 and WRs over 34 years old.

Chapter 7 When/where/how/how long is the Draft?

The draft is like Christmas day. You have your eyes on something special and you hope you get it. On draft day you are like a kid wondering what you are going to get; losing sleep the night before and the anticipation of the event building up in the weeks before it. Draft day can be that exciting!

Drafts can be live, online or over the phone. If the owners cannot be present then it is done automatically online. Live drafts are the most fun. Online drafts are more convenient but less fun. Automatic online drafts are about as fun as watching paint dry.

Draft Date

As a beginner, I recommend you try to draft as close to the start of the NFL season as possible. This way there are fewer questions about a team's starters. The ideal time for the draft would be the weekend before the NFL season starts. However, this is Labor Day weekend and some owners may be on vacation. Thus, a popular choice is after the last game of the third week of the NFL preseason. The fourth game of the NFL preseason is primarily for back-up players (no coach wants to see his starters hurt right before the season starts, so the starters usually do not play). After the third NFL preseason game you should have a good idea of the starters on each team. The later it is (closer to the NFL season kickoff), the more information you have to make informed choices. It will be a date that everyone can make. Usually this will mean a Saturday afternoon (especially if it is a live draft).

Live Draft Location

Any location that is quiet, large enough and easy to get to will work. Back yards and garages work well. In many cases the draft will be at the home of the commissioner or some owner who volunteers his abode. **No matter where it is held, make sure you get a comfortable seat, that is quiet (not beside the kitchen or**

bathroom) and have room for your materials (cheat sheets, magazine, etc.).

Think twice before offering to host the draft as a beginner. The owner of the draft house has some advantages and some disadvantages. The main advantage is the familiarity factor. He knows his house and will be comfortable in the surroundings. He will not have to drive to the draft so he can use the extra time saved (what would have been travel time to the draft) to prepare for the draft. And, perhaps most importantly, he can have the latest information from his computer right up until the other owners arrive.

The problems with being the host are the distractions that can occur if coordinating the party (food, beverages, etc.). On the day of the draft, some time will need to be spent arranging furniture and cleaning up before the guests arrive. Once the draft starts, as the host, it may be easy to get distracted by helping the guests with food, beverages, etc. Read _Fantasy Football Guidebook_ for more tips on hosting the draft.

Many leagues have moved the draft (and thus the stress) out of private homes and into public places such as a bar, restaurant or conference room. If your draft is conducted at a public place, make sure you have some privacy and are not near the band, jukebox or television. In 2009, Buffalo Wild Wings (BWW) Grill & Bar offered their restaurants as draft locations, along with offering free wings. It is an excellent place to hold a draft.

Online Drafts

In an online draft, owners draft from their own personal computers simultaneously. These are held in your home office or wherever you wish to have your computer. The same rules apply as the live draft. Minimize distractions, make the room quiet and have another computer as a backup in case the primary computer has issues. For the same reasons, **always pre-rank your players for the online draft before the draft,** that way if you get disconnected for some reason, the computer's artificial intelligence (AI) will draft players you want and not players the AI thinks you want. Often the league's initial rankings have retired, injured and suspended players ranked inappropiately.

Draft Rules

All of the draft rules below should be covered in the league constitution. Make sure that all draft rules are in writing and that you have a copy two weeks draft day. If you have a question on a rule, ask before the draft in order to get it cleared up early. **Know all the draft rules and the penalties for violating them.** Some leagues charge money, ask you to buy a round of drinks, or penalize your team with a later draft pick if you violate a draft rule. **Sometimes the penalty is so lite that violating a rule may be worth the punishment.**

Ask the commissioner if this is a friendly league (usually it will be if no serious money is on the line) or a strict league. Often in a friendly league, allowances are made for new owners. However, you do not want to look like a rookie so read below and heed.

Who Can Be Drafted

Any player not in college and eligible for the NFL can be drafted. This prevents college players from being taken before they become eligible for the NFL but does not prevent you from drafting CFL, unemployed or retired players who may make a comeback. For example, Ricky Williams was a keeper on a team in 2004 while he was retired; he then played in 2005 for that owner.

Time Limits

What about time limits to make picks? Anywhere from 1-2 minutes is normal, with 90 seconds as the most common. Don't panic! This is more than enough time if you are prepared...and you will be prepared if you follow the basic instructions outlined here. Some leagues use a clock (draftclock.com) and give a 30-second and 10-second warning before time expires. Some leagues allow less time for the first half of the draft (as an example, one minute since it is easier to make picks) and more time for the second half of the draft (possibly two minutes).

Keep in mind that the longer the time limit the longer it will take to finish the draft. For example, a 12-team league with 20 rounds would equal 240 picks. If two minutes were allowed per pick, theoretically you could be drafting for 480 minutes or over 8 hours. Most players do not take the full time, but some do and all can if they want. **A 12-team, experienced league with 20 rounds, utilizing the one and two minute time limit in the example above, can finish their draft in approximately four hours.**

What if I Miss my Pick?

Normally, if an owner does not make a pick in the time allotted, he skips his pick until the next owner drafts. Therefore, you just have to wait one pick before you get another chance at drafting. However, the time allowed for this "makeup pick" is usually only 5-10 seconds. So be ready to go when the owner after you drafts. Each subsequent time you miss the deadline you will move back a slot and get five to ten seconds to pick. Once time expires, even if you blurt out a name, you forfeit your pick until the next owner makes his pick.

What if I Pick a Player Already Chosen?

If an owner selects a player already drafted or violates the roster limits with his pick (such as maximum of three QBs and he drafts a fourth) he may be penalized. The penalty can be monetary or otherwise, or just a warning. A common penalty is deferment of their draft pick. In a friendly league, a good-natured ribbing is the worst you may expect.

Other Draft Considerations

Find out what colors the stickers are for each position on the draft board in advance of the draft. Some programs for ranking players (Draft Dominator-see Resources) allow you to customize the colors used for positions, thus giving you a jump ahead of the competition since the cheat sheet matches the colors on the draft board.

Draft Format

There are two main formats for the draft order. They are the serpentine method and the standard method. The standard method is used in specialty leagues like keeper/dynasty leagues.

Most drafts will use a serpentine method. In serpentine, the draft order reverses ("snakes back") on successive rounds. The first round would be picks 1-12, in that order. The second round would go in reverse order. Team 12 would get the first pick in round two and Team 1 (who picked first in round one) would get the last pick. Team 1 gets back-to back picks for every pick except the first and last rounds. Team 12 (or the last team in the draft) always has back-to-back picks. Odd rounds comply with the original draft order (1-12) and even rounds are the reverse (12-1). Therefore, the first four rounds would look like this: 1-12; 12-1; 1-12; 12-1. Know when your draft pick is and how many other picks are between your picks. The closer you are to the first or last draft spots, the less time you have between picks.

The other draft format is the standard draft order, which is what the NFL uses. In this case, the same draft order repeats every round. For example, the first three rounds would be 1-12, 1-12 and 1-12. Drafts for NFL rookies in FF dynasty leagues use this format the most.

Draft Order-How do I Know When I Pick?

Draft order can either be known well in advance or decided right before drafting on draft day. If the draft spots are to be known in advance, they can either be ordained by the rules (reverse order of finish from last year) or drawn at random. Leagues that use the reverse order of finish for a draft order will have the order known at the end of the season. In most cases, a new owner will be allowed to draft first. These teams will have over six months to mull over their draft spot and the strategies that go with it. It also allows more time to think about trading draft picks. If you wish to trade a draft pick, review trading in Chapter 11.

Picking draft spots at the actual draft eliminates these advantages. However, if your league waits until draft day, when everyone is present (by drawing numbers or cards out of a hat), it is hard to be challenged as to the fairness of who got what pick. It also prevents the owner who gets the last draft pick from deciding to quit (since he is drafting last and hates his draft spot). **If possible, try to play in a league where your draft spot will be** known in advance. **That way you can practice (mock draft) from that spot before the actual draft (see Chapter 8).**

Draft Day Experience

If possible, volunteer to assist with a draft before you actually draft in one. Many leagues have someone else place the labels on the board. You can ask to be this person. Placing the labels is a great way to learn some of the NFL players, teams and positions. You may have done this last year and seen how much fun the draft was and decided to join that same league this year.

Making Sure you get the Right Player

Unfortunately, there are several Smiths, Johnsons, Petersons, Claytons and Bushs in the NFL right now. So, knowing a player's last name is not enough to guarantee you get the right player. **Make sure you have the correct name and announce his full name, position and team to avoid any controversy.** You do not have to pronounce T.J Housyourmamma's name correctly. Just say TJ Houz, WR, Seattle. If you do not do this correctly, you could be stuck with Adrian Peterson of Chicago Bears fame and not the Adrian Peterson of Minnesota Viking fame. Currently there are two Steve Smith WRs, too.

Intermission

Fortunately, a draft can take four or more hours and thus at least one break is recommended. As a beginner, push for as many intermissions (10-15 minute breaks) as possible because it gives you time to recover and catch up with the draft if you fall behind. Use breaks to your advantage by updating your cheat sheets (See Appendix B Cheat Sheet Sample), mapping out strategies or examining team strengths or weaknesses. A ten-minute break in the middle to let everyone go to the bathroom seems fair. Know when the breaks are coming and, if so, do not let others push for "pressing on." Take the break to catch your breath since as a beginner you are probably farther behind than some other owner.

Summary

1. Make Draft day as close to the start of the NFL season as possible to eliminate unknowns such as starters, injuries, etc.
2. Get a comfortable draft seat. Avoid distractions at the draft such as food, noise, alcohol or visual distractions.
3. Know all the draft rules and penalites.
4. Find out your draft spot before the draft and practice (mock draft-see Chapter 8 Draft Preparation)
5. Announce the correct player's name, position and NFL team to avoid drafting the wrong Smith, Peterson, Johnson or Manning.
6. Ask for as many draft intermissions ("breaks") as possible. It helps beginners catch their breath and update their materials.

Chapter 8 How do I prepare for the Draft?

There are four major steps to draft preparation. First, you must decide on a draft strategy. This is your plan for the draft, in essence, it is what position to pick, who to pick and when to pick them. To execute this plan you will need a ranking of players at each position and an overall ranking or evaluation system. These rankings are commonly called cheat sheets (See Appendix B Cheat Sheet Sample). Next, create a cheat sheet for your draft. Third, you must gather your draft materials together. No, it is not just your cheat sheets but also much more. Finally, practice drafting as much as possible to get a feel for how it happens.

Draft Strategy (Have a Plan)

There is an old saying that goes "If you fail to prepare, you prepare to fail." Have a plan. Who do I draft and when? This plan will be based on your draft strategy. There are several strategies from which to choose. The most common is the Stud RB theory. The Stud WR theory has also gained some followers due to the growing running back by committee (RBBC) situations in the NFL. Value-based drafting (VBD) is an advanced theory and beyond the scope of this book. (See _Fantasy Football Guidebook_.)

The Stud RB theory suggests that you draft 2 RBs in the first 3 rounds of the draft. RBs are in limited supply and the demand for them is so great that getting RBs early and often is a good idea (see Appendix A, Supply and Demand Table). The Stud WR theory goes even further and suggests drafting two WRs with the first two picks of the draft. In essence, it states that the top WRs are dependable so get them first, then aquire RBs later. The Stud WR theory is most often employed with the later draft spots (11th or 12th) since you can get two top 5 WRs with back to back picks to start the draft. VBD suggests using your overall cheat sheet and drafting the best players available for the first 10 rounds or so. Unfortunately, this can lead to multiple TEs or QBs at the expense of RBs and WRs unless you fully understand what VBD is based on. Therefore, I do not recommend VBD for beginners.

For a beginner I recommend forgoing all of these theories and instead use either a simple "Stud at each postion theory" or the harder "stockpile RBs and WRs theory".

Easy Draft Plan - Stud at Each Position

The easiest plan is to draft a stud at each of the major positions (QB, RB, WR and TE). In this case, **you want to get a top 5 player at each of the four important player positions**. You are sacrificing strength at RB and WR in general because you must draft a RB2 and WR2 much later, but you gain by having more strength at QB1 and TE1. Why this plan? It makes your start/sit decisions each week much easier if you have a clear player who should start at these positions. It is a no brainer that each will be your starter every week unless they are hurt or on a bye week.

To do this you will need to go into the draft with a plan of drafting a RB, then WR, then QB, then TE. So rounds 1-4 will be:
Round 1   RB
Round 2   WR
Round 3   QB
Round 4   TE
In rounds 5-8 you then draft 2 more RBs and WRs. So, after round 8 you have 1 QB, 3 RBs, 3WRs, 1 TE. You have all of your starting positions filled (except K and Def which you will draft at the end of the draft). Round 9 will be WR in order to have a WR to step in for bye weeks from your WR1, WR2 and WR3. Later rounds will be back ups (QB2, TE2, etc.) but you can wait on them since you have a top QB1 and TE1. No need to waste too high a pick on your backups there. Wait until the third round from the last to draft your defense, then kicker with the next to last pick and then get a player with your last pick that you need (bye weeks messed up at another position, or that you hope will be a sleeper (see Chapter 6)). (See Appendix E - Easy Draft Plan)

Hard Draft Plan - Stockpile RBs and WRs

A more difficult draft plan to implement is the "stockpile RBs and WRs (also known as the wait on QBs and TEs) plan (See Appendix F). With this plan, you draft 3 RBs and 3 WRs with your first six draft choices. Usually they are evenly distributed (like RB-WR-RB-WR-RB-WR or WR-RB-RB-WR-RB-WR). Your seventh pick is a WR. You wait on QB and TE until round 8 or later. Your roster is essentially the same as the easy draft plans, but the quality of your QB and TE is such that another QB or TE is needed in the next round or two. Therefore, after 11 rounds you have 2 QBs. 3 RBs, 4 WRs and 2 TEs. You have fewer but better RBs and WRs than the easy plan.

Handcuff (HC)

Plan to handcuff your first RB drafted. This means drafting his backup later in the draft. You may want to HC your RB2 depending on how good he is and how good his backup may be. Do not handcuff your QB unless his backup is just as good or better, if given the opportunity, or unless he is injury prone. In 2010, Matt Leinart should be given the starting job in Arizona, but his position is not tenable and the WRs there are so good that it makes his backup a worthy HC option. But only as your QB3. In other words, have another starting QB on your team to fill in for the bye week and if you can afford it, keep the HC QB as your QB3. **Do not HC WRs or TEs**. WRs should be drafted on their merits alone and only occassionally will the option of having a backup WR, on the bench, who does not start, be feasible.

Cheat Sheets

Cheat sheets (See Appendix B) consist of players ranked from best to worst at each position based on projected fantasy points for the upcoming season. In other words, the projected highest scoring QB will be ranked first and then the next highest scoring QB and so on, based on what you think they will do in the season ahead. **Be careful about projections, sometimes the player with the most TDs will not always be ranked #1.** Each position should be ranked with as many players that could be drafted. If possible, look at last year's draft in your league and use that as an estimate of how many QBs, RBs, etc. will be drafted and make sure you have that many, and a few more, in your rankings. As a minium, have 30

QBs, 60 RBs, 60 WRs, 30 TEs, 30 K and 32 DEF ranked on your cheat sheets. **More teams means more players drafted.**

Another vital ranking on your cheat sheets needs to be an overall ranking of the top 100-200 players. This serves as a "best of" list and you can use it to draft the best RB or WR when faced with that choice. Be careful though, as overall rankings usually place kickers and defenses too high since they score so many points. However, since both positions have little differences between the 3rd player and the 20th player, wait and draft them in the late rounds. **Use your overall rankings early in the draft for the best available player (until about round 10 or 11) and then use the positional rankings to fill needs.** For example, "I need a kicker so who is the best one left."

Cheat sheets are like taking your notes into an open book test in school. They help you decide what is right and what is wrong and you want the best information on them. Just as you did when taking those final exams, highlight important information (players you really want (sleepers for example) so that it is easy to see in the heat of the moment. If the cheat sheets are so messy that you cannot undertsand what the information is, that does not help you. So make sure that your cheat sheets have player's names, NFL team names and especially bye weeks. The team names will prevent you from mistakenly drafting all players from the same NFL team.

The same goes with the bye weeks. **Avoid having your starter and his backup on the same bye weeks.** For example, if both of your QBs are out in week seven on a bye week, then who will be your starter? At best, you will have to drop another player and add a QB for that week to fill in. He will not be the best if he is still leftover after the draft. In the worst-case scenario, there are no starting QBs left over or you cannot afford to drop another player to add a QB for that week, in which case your team gets ZERO points at QB that week.

When faced with a choice of drafting a player from the same position with the same bye week, just skip the player and draft the next best player at that position with a different bye week. The next player should not be much less productive in terms of fantasy points.

The fantasy points (FP) projected should be based on your league's scoring system. If they are not based on your scoring system, then you are comparing apples to oranges when it comes time to draft. The scoring system used to rank players must be the same as your league scoring rules or very close in order to have good rankings. How do you get the rankings?

Rankings can be done in many different ways. There is one easy way and that is to use a premium service like _www.Footballguys.com._ I discuss them in detail in Chapter 12 - Resources. If you pay for their services, you can get rankings for the draft and each week for starters based on your exact scoring system. The cheat cheats they provide are easy to read and use. Footballguys.com provides several formats for cheat sheets: you can download a software program called Draft Dominator that lets you practice drafting and allows customizable cheat sheets or simply print out a pre-made cheat sheet based on many of the most common scoring systems around.

Another easy way is to use a pre-printed magazine cheat sheet (or one provided by your league website). However, make sure it is updated prior to your draft. So if you bought a copy of _FF Index magazine_ or _FF Pro Forecast_ magazine (see Chapter 12 Resources), you could use their cheat sheets (which are outdated since they came out in July) and simply update them by replacing players who have retired, been injured, promoted/demoted, etc.

The hard way to do rankings is to do them on your own. If you go this route, I recommend picking up a copy of _Fantasy Football Guidebook_ since I go into more detail in that book about doing your own rankings. But if you insist on going this route, here is a quick method. Rank each position seperately.

1) Start with last year's statistics (based on fantasy points scored, if available) with as many players ranked as you think will go in the draft (see minimums earlier).

2) Replace any players who have retired or been suspended for the year. Their replacements may not be as good, or as bad, but this is a good starting point.

3) Look at the number of games played for each player. If less than 16, move them up to where they would have been had they played all 16 games. So if a WR has 150 FPs and only played 12 of 16

games, assume he will score 200 next year and move him up accordingly.

Expected FPs = (16/# games played) x Fantasy Points from last year

4) Do the reverse for any players currently expected to miss games due to injury or suspension. **For injured players, add an extra game missed simply because they will not be at 100% right away.** So, if a player is expected to miss the first 2 games due to an injury, use 3 games out.

Expected FPs = (16 - # of games missing/16) x Fantasy Points from last year

Same WR who we expected to score 200 in a full season is now projected to be 162.5.
5) Add rookies and other player movements by looking at the team's depth charts. If a rookie is supposed to start right away, then he will knock the old veteran down or out of your ranking. If a team adds another good WR, that may decrease the existing WRs points.
6) Account for team upgrades/downgrades. If a team improves at QB, bump up the WRs a bit, if the OL improves move the RB up and vice versa. A new head coach who changes the way the offense is run can also change expected points from players, both positively and negatively.
7) Once your preliminary rankings are done, compare them to others. If any player is very high or very low relatively speaking, re-evaluate.
8) The last step is to use your gut. Look at your rankings and move players up or down a little bit based on what you think will happen this season, based on what you have read, heard or seen.

Miscellaneous Tips for Player Rankings by Position

QB

1) Avoid rookie QBs, QBs on new teams or with new systems
2) Losing teams can have good fantasy QBs
3) Know the rules. Do fumbles and interceptions count against them?
4) OL woes can hurt a good QBs production

RB

1) Favor teams that win more games; they have more game-ending rushing drives. Teams that are behind often go to the passing option.
2) Avoid if injury-prone
3) Look at age and number of touches (carries and receptions) he gets each year
4) The more backup RBs (as opposed to WRs or TEs) stockpiled on your team, the better chance of one becoming a starter

WR

1) Losing teams can have good WRs, especially in PPR leagues as the teams behind must play catchup by passing.
2) Few WR2s should be ranked ahead of any teams WR1.
3) Avoid rookies except for the first WR chosen in the NFL draft. But look to youth in the late rounds for your WR sleepers.
4) The more WRs on your team, the better chance of one becoming a starter.
5) Avoid WRs limping into the season with an injury; the risk is too great.
6) Choose WRs with good or great QBs.

TE

1) Talent drops off after TE12. Any TE from TE1 through TE12 is worth owning. After that, they are not worth much FP wise.
2) Draft before K or DEF but after starting RBs and WRs
3) Avoid rookie TEs, but upgrade those with rookie QBs. These QBs tend to dump passes off to their safety valve the TE.
4) Look for 3rd year TEs drafted in the 1st and 2nd round of the NFL draft. *Fantasy Football Almanac* lists the previous five years NFL draft data.

Easiest Way to Predict a Breakout WR

1)   Take the top 2 WRs from each team that had a Top 15 QB last year (2 x 15=30).
2)   Eliminate some teams because last year was a fluke. They may have played a very easy schedule or their Top 15 QB may have left the team. If this was the case, remove those WRs. With this discriminator, you will lose an average of six WRs. (30-6 players =24 WRs)
3)   Remove any WRs on this list who were in the Top 15 WRs last year. Everyone knows about them and they will be ranked high. 24-15=9.
4)   Of the remaining WRs, the ones in their 2nd-5th season are your candidates. The more experienced they are (5th year being the most experienced), the higher they should be ranked. This usually results in 6-8 breakout WR candidates (See Appendix G for 2010 WR predictions).

The steps above are a good start for a beginner who wants to create their own rankings. You can do the same technique at each position to find players who are unnoticed but have the potential to breakout. But what about the overall rankings? How do you know whether RB20 is more valuable or WR25? The overall rankings will tell you this, but it is based on many factors, including how many teams are in the league, the scoring system, the roster size for teams and the starter requirements. For a beginner, I recommend using an overall cheat sheet from a FF magazine based on the same scoring, # of teams, roster size and starting rosters as your FF league. But use it simply to create a blank overall ranking based on position. (I.e. ignore the names on the overall sheet that is perfect for your league, use the ordering of positions.) For example, ranking 1-8 is RB, then 2 WRs, then 3 RBs, and so on until you have 120 positions listed. Now go back and fill in names based on YOUR rankings. So, the first RB on your RB rankings goes in the first RB spot on the overall cheat sheet. The 5th TE on your TE rankings will go in the overall rankings wherever the 5th TE is listed. The idea here is that someone else has figured out the relationships between the RB20 and WR25 and you use that information combined with who you think is the 20th best RB and the 25th best WR.

Materials

What do you need to draft? The first thing is those cheat sheets we just discussed. They are a must. If possible, try and get them so that they are compact. The overall rankings could be on one page and the RB and WR on another page, finishing up with QB, TE, K and DEF on the last page. Who is playing on each bye week is critical, so I put the bye weeks at the top of my overall cheat sheet and write in each NFL team corresponding to the bye week.

Another essential piece of information is the NFL schedule. A single piece of paper should have the entire regular season on it. Highlight the teams that play the worst teams during the bye weeks and the fantasy playoffs weeks. This gives you a quick reference when you are on the draft clock as to which teams have the best matchups those weeks. So far we have 4 pieces of paper: 3 cheat sheets and an NFL schedule. Consider bringing a FF magazine or *Fantasy Football Almanac* (mentioned in Chapter 12 Resources) to hide your cheat sheets from prying eyes and as a crutch in case you lose some of your materials. *Fantasy Football Almanac* also has the NFL schedule so it can cover that angle for you too.

Do not even think about bringing a laptop to the draft unless you are proficeint enough to work it and draft at the same time. Most of us are not. Do bring several pencils so that you can line through the names of the players on your cheat sheets as they are drafted by other owners. Avoid using pens because, inevitably, some owner will make a mistake and then you cannot erase your mark through that player if you used a pen. **Circle the players that you draft so that you can see their names, teams, positions and bye weeks easily.** Do not mark through your own players names and bye weeks.

Mock Drafts

Practice, practice, practice…you have heard that drilled into your head since you were a child. Practice does make perfect, especially when dealing with something as fluid as a FF draft. No two drafts are the same. By practicing you will be better prepared for the unexpected. If you have never participated in a draft, simply practicing once will give you a much better appreciation for the tasks ahead. But how do you practice drafting?

Mock drafts are practice drafts. They can occur with other humans as the other owners or with a computer's artificial intelligence (AI) acting as one or more of the owners. If you want to face some human competition, sites like Mock Draft Central www.mockdraftcentral.com offer free and easy mock drafts. FootballDiehards.com has a great mock draft website too. It is at http://www.footballdiehards.com/MockDraft. Software progams like Draft Dominator from www.footballguys.com have functions that you can use by yourself to mock draft. In all instances, make sure the rules (scoring, # of teams, roster size, starters, etc.) are as close to your league rules as possible. Don't be afraid. The mock drafts do not count; they are simply a way to practice different strategies or to get a feel for what a draft is like. Thomas Jefferson once said, "I am a great believer in luck, and I find the harder I work, the more I have of it." Obviously, he was not refering to FF, but it applies to mock drafts. The more you do, the better you will be.

How to Have a Good Draft (or What Not to Do)

1) Be prepared. When I say this, I mean have your materials ready, and know who is retired, suspended, in the hospital, in the pokey, and generally collecting an NFL paycheck. Know the rules for starter positions (i.e do you start 2 RBs or 3 RBs). I hate to see owners draft two TEs only to realize we are a TE-optional league. This also means cell phones off unless you are getting updates for the draft.

2) If you have a co-owner, work out who does what in advance, discuss strategy in advance and talk about the players you want, need, and absolutely will not draft. Arm wrestling over whether the team should select Terrell Owens (WR) on draft day does not a fun afternoon make.

3) Don't lose track of when it is your turn or who else has been picked. Some leagues penalize you when you pick a player

already picked. Track who is drafted ahead of you; cross their name off your lists and move on with your life. Get over it.

4) Do not drink and draft. There is a good reason they give out free booze in Las Vegas.

5) Show up on time (early if possible). Nothing starts the league off worse than the 1 p.m. draft starting at 1:45 p.m. If you are going to be late, give good instructions to your most trusted confidant so that they can draft for you. When you do show up, do not complain about their picks; they are only as good as the guidance you provided.

6) Leave the children at home. They will not enjoy watching you draft, nor will the other owners enjoy babysitting for you while you decide between Reggie Bush and Joseph Addai.

7) Do not look at other people's draft lists unless they invite you to. Returning from the draft with a black eye only serves to make your spouse suspicious.

8) Do not go to the bathroom right before your pick. See #4 above about no drinking. No fluid, no tinkle.

9) Let the commissioner run things. If he asks you to do your loud attention-gathering whistle, fine. Other than that it is his show.

Summary

1) Have a Strategy (plan)
a) Easy – RB, WR, QB and then a TE (Appendix E) or
b) Hard – 3 RBs and 3 WRs and a QB and TE later (Appendix F)
2) Handcuff (HC) your RB1 and maybe RB2.
3) Cheat sheets are a must.
4) Gather your materials and be ready for the draft.
5) Participate in mock drafts to get experience.

Chapter 9 Who should I start each week?

As the owner of the team, you must set a starting lineup for each week. You decide which of the players on your team will start (i.e. be the ones to add points to your team) and which will sit on the bench (not add points to your team). The number of starters, and from which position is determined by the rules for your league (see Chapter 4). In many leagues, starters will be 1 QB, 2 RBs, 3 WRs, 1 TE, 1 K and 1 DEF/ST. Some leagues may also have a flex player who can be a RB, WR or TE. In the scenario above, with three WR starters and a flex player, you must name 10 players as starters. Your starting lineup decisions decide the winners and losers in each week's H2H matchup. It is the points scored weekly from submitting starting lineups that determines who wins each week and ultimately, which fantasy teams make the playoffs for your league.

Most leagues now have their own point projection service that attempts to predict how many points a player will score for the week and, in some stat services, for the next few weeks or remainder of the season. If this is the case, evaluate the system after the first week (since those starters are pretty much your first draft picks) and perhaps use it for the entire season. No system is perfect so do not be too hard on the predictor. Things to look for: **how often is it updated (Does it know when a player has been declared out for the game on Sunday?), how far off are the predictions from the results (Does it predict too many points or too little points in most cases?) and what does it use to calculate points (Does it use your league rules or is it another scoring system?).**

Quite possibly the best lineup advice is to watch the football games (and the pregame shows); especially for the Sunday early games, Sunday and Monday Night games and any Thursday or Saturday games. Sometimes breaking news is revealed just before kickoff and can affect your lineup decisions. For example, Player B will miss the game due to a death in his family, or suspension, etc. Perhaps you are starting Player B; now you can bench him and start someone else in his place. You can save yourself some missed FPs by staying on top of the action right before the game starts. Perhaps your WR was catching passes from QB B, now QB X will be tossing those passes to him this week. Maybe you will want to rethink your lineup decisions based on QB X at quarterback.

In week 16 of 2009, I had Steven Jackson as a starter. He was listed as questionable (as he had been for the past few weeks), but always played. So I forgot to check his status for the 4 pm game. He did not play in week 16. I found out too late to replace him. It was the difference between finishing 10th out of 228 top competitors in the Fantasy Football Players Championship (www.theFFPC.com) and 16th. It was a huge mistake.

Most information about players comes out 30 minutes prior to game time.

Who Do I Start (WDIS)?

WDIS decisions (also known as start 'em or sit 'em decisions) are perhaps the hardest choices in the fantasy season. The draft is a one-time event, the consequences of which can be changed with trades or free agent acquisitions(see Chapters 10 and 11). Start/sit decisions are made week after week throughout the season and can drive an owner crazy. Ultimately, the right WDIS decision last week can be the wrong decision this week, or vice versa. The worst situation is where regardless what you decide, it always turns out to be wrong. Your teams performance suffers when you start the least performing players, and a sense of self-doubt creeps in. Sometimes the hardest decision you may have is benching a player and starting someone else. As John Madden said about start/bench decisions: "It is a lot easier to stand pat than make a change." If you have a method for determining who to start, these decisions can be easier. Therefore, you need an easy to follow method to answer the question "who do I start". How about a checklist to follow for start/sit decisions? Is it 100% full proof? No. Is it a great start that will work 80% of the time? Yes. In addition, it is a tool you can use initially until you have some experience playing FF, at which time you can modify the WDIS Checklist to include techniques you have learned. Refer to *Fantasy Football Guidebook* for a detailed explanation of the start/sit process and *Fantasy Football Tips* for more on WDIS decisions.

The order of these steps is important. Later steps should generally not override earlier steps.

Rule #1 – Always set a lineup; (remember early week Thursday and Saturday games)

I know it sounds simple enough, always set a lineup. However, a typical rookie mistake is not setting a lineup (it can happen to anyone). Set a lineup each week even if you are on a cruise ship or on a bus trip. If you know you will be incommunicado (away from the internet), set your lineup early in the week using the best information available. That way you gave your fantasy team a fighting chance.

The best plan is to set aside 30 minutes before the first game (from 12:30 PM EST on Sunday) to check the weather and injury issues for your players and set a lineup based on this information. Not setting a lineup makes the other owners mad because they may need you to beat your opponent. Do not make that mistake. **Set your lineup for next week as soon as possible; if nothing else, bench bye week players and make substitutions based on injuries.** You can always change it later. Better to have a serviceable lineup in case you get hit by a Guinness beer truck and miss the deadline. This means you need to know your deadline. Remember Thursday games. Do it on Wednesday at the latest for your initial hack at lineups. Luckily, most leagues use the rule that last week's lineup is automatically used for this coming week until changed. In this case, you will always have a lineup, but it may not be the one you want until you actually change it.

Some league management systems allow owners to set their lineups for each week individually before the start of the season. If this is the case, use it before the season starts to bench your bye week players during their off week. Use the next best player at that position to replace him for the week. It is a great reminder.

Rule #2 – Always begin this WDIS process with your top picks from the draft

This is probably as easy as it is going to get. Start the players you drafted first. Because you drafted them higher, you must think they are better than those drafted later. So in week 1 start the first QB you drafted. Unless an injury or can't-miss matchup occurs in week 1 (see steps below), the first RB drafted goes into RB#1 position, second RB drafted goes into RB#2, and so on.

Rule #3 – Always start your studs

Your studs will be your top 3-4 draft picks. Therefore, they will be your RB1 and WR1 and maybe RB2 or WR2 and thus a Top 10 RB or WR (if using the Stockpile RBs and WRs plan). If you use the easy drafting plan from Chapter 8, then your studs will be your RB1, WR1, QB1 and TE1. There is a reason why studs were drafted that high. Chris Johnson (RB, TEN) and Peyton Manning (QB, IND) should never be benched unless they are on a bye week or are hurt and thus doubtful or out for the game (or unless they lose their job; fat chance).

Why? Simple – they are your highest scoring players (that is why you drafted them so high in the first place) and thus they will score the most for you over the season. Do not worry about matchups. They are going to provide you big points if you start them week in and week out. **Start them and forget about them**. Only bench a stud if he is hurt, suspended or has nothing to play for and is expected to not finish the game. The day you bench one because he is playing against the best defense is the day he scores three TDs and has a career high day. Trying to time their big games is like trying to time the stock market. DON'T DO IT. Consider your studs your index mutual funds and let them ride. If the stud has a slow start or a game or two below average, rest assured that he will return to the mean eventually. You just do not want to have him on your bench when he does. If you try to time the big games and the bad games you will be burned more times than not, so start them regardless. You will not lose sleep by starting your studs and them having an off day.

Rule #4 – Never start a player on a bye

During the course of the season, the NFL gives each team a week off, called their bye week. If your player is not playing in a given week then you will need to replace him as a starter. Bye weeks mean shuffling players from the bench to fill gaps left open as your normal starters are not playing. In 2009, bye weeks meant that weeks 4-10 saw an absence of some teams. Most weeks only had four teams on a bye, but weeks 7, 8 and 9 had six teams on a bye. Those weeks, known as "black Sundays," had owners really scrambling to field a team as 6 of the 32 possible starting RBs and QBs stayed home and watched football on TV. Therefore, if you were in a 14-team league that started two RBs, somebody did not have a starter. (32-6=26 playing RBs; 2 x 14=28 needed). It gets even worse when you factor in a flex position. There were quite a few teams with WRs as flex players in those weeks.

Rule #5 –   Do not start doubtful or out players

The NFL has four terms it asks head coaches to use in categorizing injuries. They are:

PROBABLE (P) - the player has a 75% chance of playing.

QUESTIONABLE (Q) - the player has a 50% chance of playing.

DOUBTFUL (D) -(you guessed it) the player has a 25% chance of playing that week.

The last term is **OUT** and that means he will not play that week. Caveat: there have been a few rare instances where a player is listed as OUT but played anyway. Teams and coaches can get into big trouble if this happens because they are required to provide information to the betting public and bad information may alter the odds in one way or another. Therefore, if a team says a player is "OUT," you can trust them on that. This is not to say that you should believe the other three terms without any question.

Normally, this information will be available on your league website in the form of injury news or with a symbol, letter or note beside the player's name on your team roster page. Pay close attention to these notes as they can give you valuable information concerning the status of a player. Injury reports are fluid lists. They change from Wednesday to Friday to Saturday to Sunday morning to game time, so be wary of some of the information. Some coaches may list an injury and say it is more serious than it is, hoping his opponents do not plan for that player. Others underestimate the injury so that opponents waste time preparing for that player. Tennessee head coach Jeff Fisher has a habit of listing every player who is even slightly hurt as questionable or out every week.

CBS, Fox and ESPN all have a ticker on their pre-game shows that tells the weather and injury status for each of the games. **If a player is listed as OUT, bench him immediately and replace him using this checklist.** The same goes for injured players listed as DOUBTFUL. Do this as soon as you find out their status. If you wait, you may forget to do it. Will a doubtful player play in some cases? YES. However, this checklist is designed to be simple and easy, **so remember if in doubt, bench him.**

Missing a game is different from "not starting a game." Do not overreact to news that your player is not starting. Sometimes coaches will not start a player due to their tardiness to a team meeting or some other infraction. It is the coach's way of instilling some discipline. The player will not be announced as the starter and may miss the first series, but if he is a stud player (and he should be if he is on your team and starting) then he will get his playing time. In fact, he may have a great game trying to impress the coaches that he disappointed or angered earlier.

Rule #6 – After week 4 start hot players and bench cold players

Look at how many points your players have scored in the past weeks and use that as a measure of value. If your WR has scored in four straight games, why take him out (at least think about starting him)? Let him ride until he produces a zero, then evaluate why he did not produce. WRs, especially once they connect with a QB on a TD several games in a row, can have a connection that lasts a long time. Statistical trends will start to break out after the first few weeks (weeks 4-5). Watch QBs and RBs early. If they are off to a slow start after the first three games, they are unlikely to do well for the rest of the season. (Exceptions to this rule are the top studs in QBs and RBs or if the team they played had tough defenses.)

Some WRs start slower than others but are usually able to recover. With a QB or RB, if they are well below their average after week 3, you may have reason to panic. Look for trends (hot streaks). QBs like to throw to the same people. If your WR3 on the bench has caught a TD the past four games, you might consider moving him into the WR2 position if he has scored more over that time than your current WR2. If a RB fumbles early (especially rookies), he may be benched. If he does well, a coach will ride him until he cools off or for the entire season if he does well.

Look for trends, not one game wonders. Anyone can look special against bad teams. How they scored their FPs is equally important. Was it garbage time statistics? Garbage time is the end of the game when one team is so far behind that the other team lets them move down the field because doing so uses up the remaining game time. It can produce great stats but garbage time is unpredictable. Watch out for fluke plays that increase stats too. A RB with 13 carries for 99 yards looks impressive, until you dig deeper and discover he had 12 carries for 5 yards and one missed tackle led to another carry for 94 yards. In this case, he is not performing as well as his statistics indicate. This can fool you into thinking he is better than he really is.

Rule #7 – Bench players in heavy rain, snow or swirling/gusty winds

How can you tell what the weather will be for the game? Your league website should have this information. In some cases, it will be a separate column with the games and weather listed. On the other hand, it may be a symbol that signals a weather advisory or note for that player due to the weather. In many instances, the notes and information about the player's upcoming game may mention the inclement weather. Finally, CBS, FOX and ESPN all have tickers at the bottom of their NFL TV programs to announce weather conditions and sometimes even a weather forecaster on the show to discuss the topic.

Bad weather usually hurts the offensive players and helps the defensive players. But bad weather needs to be defined as heavy rain, heavy snow or swirling or gusting winds. Of course, domes neutralize whatever the outside weather is so if your player is playing in a dome you can ignore the weather concerns. Here are the dome stadiums: St. Louis, Arizona, Atlanta, New Orleans, Detroit, Minnesota, Dallas, Houston and Indianapolis. Note most are in the NFC.

Winds will affect QBs, WRs and kickers. Swirling winds are the worst. If it is a constant wind from the same direction, QBs and kickers can compensate, but when the wind changes direction and speed frequently, all bets are off; unless of course your defense is playing there, then that is a good thing!

Do not be too worried about snow. Many WRs love snow because they know where they are going and can use it to their advantage. However, be wary of heavy snow since this will affect the ability of the QBs and kickers to put the ball a long way down field. Rain is the most difficult weather condition to take into account. The effect it has on vision is probably most dramatic, as a heavy downpour limits down field views.

Warmer temperatures can affect players too. Extreme heat (90 degrees or higher) tends to help the offense, and extreme cold (20 degrees and below) helps the defense.

Therefore, bench players playing in heavy rain, heavy snow or swirling, gusting winds as the chances are high that their production will be reduced.

Rule #8 – Avoid good defenders and tough defenses

Avoid starting players whose NFL opponents are exceptionally good defenders. A few defensive players in the NFL are known as "Shut Down" (SD) corners (safeties). These corners are so good that they "shut down" anyone they are assigned to cover. Your WR and even perhaps the QB throwing to him can have poor days against these great defenders. Darelle Revis of the

NYJ is one. Champ Bailey of DEN is another. Avoid starting players against the SD corners. This may be one case where rule #3 - Always start your studs is overruled (especially for WRs). Usually the team's best cornerback faces the offense's best WR.

Look at a defense's rushing yardage allowed, passing yardage allowed and points allowed. Tough defenses allow few yards and points and thus few fantasy points. FPs allowed per position by a defense is a common tool used to determine who to start. If a defense gives up lots of points to TEs in general, then your TE should have a good day.

Start your QB, WR and TE against defenses weak agaisnt the pass. Start your RBs against defenses weak versus the rush. Think twice about starting RBs versus defenses they cannot rush on. Think twice about starting your QB, WR or TE against defenses they cannot pass on.

Look for the most favorable matchup. Start defenses that are at home, against poor offenses and/or inexperienced QBs. Start QBs against weak passing defenses or teams with strong offenses. The QB will be playing from behind and thus is more likely to throw. If two teams are meeting for the second time in a season, look back at what happened in their previous meeting. Did one QB have a great day statistically? Was it high scoring? Did the kickers kick many FGs while the offenses struggled? Does a certain player always seem to "get up" for a game versus this opponent? Look at games in the previous year. Rivalries can be great matchups.

Speaking of rivalries, look for special events that will motivate players or teams to do better. For example, Brett Favre returns to face the team that fired him (GB) as a Minnesota Vikings QB and throws 4 TDs and 244 yards or Carson Palmer and Marvin Lewis giving a "put up or shut up" speech and Cincinnati beats New Orleans 31-16 at New Orleans after losing three straight games.

Rule #9 – Use Las Vegas odds to help with close calls

Use the Las Vegas odds for the lesser player (WR, K, and DEF) decisions. Consider kickers. If you have a choice between two kickers, who do you start? First, look at the Las Vegas odds for

both games they are playing. Matt Prater is one kicker as Denver
plays Oakland. The other kicker is David Akers as Philadelphia
plays Washington. Look at the over/under and then who is favored
in both games.

Den -3 Oak +3 O/U 37
Phil -7 Wash +7 O/U 47

For those unfamiliar with these terms, Denver is favored to
win by 3 points. Philadelphia is favored to win by 7 points. The
over/under refers to how many total points (TPs) both teams are
expected to score in the game. The higher the over/under, the
higher scoring is expected. If a player's team is in a higher scoring
game and they are favored by a large margin, then Las Vegas
expects their team to score the most points.

The bookies expect Denver to win 20-17 and expect
Philadelphia to win 27-20. David Akers (PHI) should have one
more extra point than Matt Prater (DEN). Obviously, the bookies
do not know exactly what will happen but they do odds for a living
and thus the over/under should be quite accurate. The over/under
says that they expect Philadelphia to score more points than Denver
because Philadelphia is favored by more points and the over/under
is higher for their game. All else being equal go with Akers today. If
you need to decide between two equal players who will just be a bye
week fill-in, choose the player scheduled to play in the higher
scoring game (higher over/under score). Be sure to look at the
amount a favored team is predicted to win by. There may be
instances when a lower over/under game will provide a higher team
score because of the lopsidedness of the predicted victory margin.

Rule #10 – Tiebreakers for Toss-Ups

Use the following only if you have used other methods
(such as Las Vegas odds or weather) to determine who to start and
you have two or three players who are all about the same and you
do not know who to start. The first discriminator is home field
advantage. If they are all equal, the players at home should have a
little advantage. That is why the NFL odds-makers give roughly 3
points to the home team in their odds assessments. So, go with the
home player. He has had better sleep, has not had to travel and is

playing in front of his hometown crowd. Do not forget that Dallas, Pittsburgh and Green Bay have many fans that travel to away games. Sometimes when they are on the road it is hard to tell who is the home team by crowd reaction.

If both are at home, neither are, or that was what made them a toss-up to begin with, then go with whichever will be playing on a nationally televised game. Why? Because now they get to showcase themselves to the nation. Most players feel a little extra excitement about playing on national TV and this should give them a slight edge over other players. They will be bringing their "A" game for the Thursday, Saturday, Sunday or Monday Night viewing audience. If that is not a factor, use the player you will be able to watch on TV where you live. Obviously, this does not help that player play any better, but at least you can get the satisfaction of watching him perform. I would much rather watch my kicker kick FGs live than to nervously watch the two-minute ticker and wonder how long each FG was or if the 6 points they scored was a missed extra point or two FGs. Go with the player on your TV set (unless you have Direct TV and NFL Sunday Ticket, where this dilemma becomes moot).

The last decision is to start the player who plays in the latest game. This gives you the opportunity to have a chance to win the longest (this simply lets you be in the game and delays the fat lady singing). There is nothing worse than having all of your players play in the early game and seeing that you lost after three hours. I would much rather have a player or two in the second Sunday game and know that I still have a chance to win, however feeble. Even better would be players on the Sunday or Monday night game, but they should already have been chosen with the above discriminators. This again is not some magical formula for providing the maximum fantasy points; it is merely a preferred method for extending the joy of fantasy football.

Checklist for Toss-Up Starter Decisions

1) Go with home team players first (QBs, K and DEF play slightly better at home)

2) Choose those playing in national TV game

3) Choose a player playing in a game you can watch

4) Choose a player playing in the latest game (4 p.m. EST or Sunday Night or Monday Night Football)

As you can imagine, there will be some gut wrenching decisions during the season. For example, my stud RB is on a bye, so who do I start? Start the next best backup (start with your first backup RB drafted unless an injury or matchup begs for another RB). For more detailed strategies, see *Fantasy Football Guidebook*.

Summary

1. See Appendix H for WDIS Checklist.
2. Watch the pregame shows - most information on player status comes out 30 minutes before game time.
3. Extreme heat favors offense. Extreme cold favors defense.
4. The checklist for tiebreakers (See Appendix I) is more for fun, less about FPs.

Chapter 10 How do I improve my Team through Free Agency?

A typical rookie mistake is not making any moves after the draft. Even if you have a successful draft, your work is not over. At some point in the season, you will have a team need. Maybe one TE is on a bye and the other is hurt. In that case, you need a TE for the week. **There are three ways to fill a need: from your bench, free agency or through a trade (approach a need in that order).** The easiest way to meet a need is through your own bench. If that is not possible, then free agency may be an option. The best (most successful) owners try to improve their team, or at best, block their opponent from improving their team via free agency. For every owner that drafts a great team, another has a weak draft but makes some great in-season additions to make the playoffs. We all make mistakes at the draft. We may be able to fix these mistakes through free agency upgrades and trades. Free agency is easier than trading because free agency does not involve another owner, but the free agent pool sometimes does not have the talent you need. In those cases, a trade may be your only option. (See Chapter 11 – Trades.)

Things happen that force you to make changes. Many owners will not conduct any transactions early in the year because they still have faith in their drafted team. This is a good strategy as it takes a few weeks for trends to develop. It is better to wait a few weeks than to be hasty with dropping key players on a slump. An **easy beginner step is to wait until week 4 before making major moves that impact your starters**. Still other owners will rarely make changes unless forced to by injuries. Look at the statistical leaders each week and see if any were not drafted. If available, look at them more closely. Are they getting the touches only because the star is hurt but will be back soon, are they coming in and replacing the star because of his nagging injuries, or is it an RBBC and the star is losing the battle? By observing the box score/stat leader boards and doing some research, you can beat other owners to the punch on these up-and-coming players. **Remember: never accept**

the status quo; always try to improve your team. At the same time, you need to be careful not to drop your up- and-coming players for the "flavor of the week" (i.e. players who have done very well in the latest week of competition but have not shown other indications of greatness).

Formats

All players not on a roster at any given time are either on the FA list or on the waiver wire. The waiver wire is for players recently dropped and awaiting processing onto the FA list. Usually a player must stay on waivers for a certain amount of time (2-3 days); during which if another owner requests him and wins (has a higher priority or bids the most FAAB), he can be claimed at the end of the waiver period. Any player not claimed off waivers will go to the FA list. The FA listing includes players who are free (hence the name) to be picked up by the first owner who requests them. Another format requires that all players be claimed off waivers, so none are readily available. Some leagues use the FA list and waiver wire as the same vehicle. These leagues use a waiver wire priority to determine who can claim a player.

Free Agency Upgrade

Free Agent Types

There are two types of players to pick up in free agency. Those who will be used just for one week to fill a bye week or suspension gap and those that will be added as a permanent member of your fantasy team. So, there are short-term adds and long-term adds. **The short-term free agents (STFA) can be picked using the methods in Chapter 9 Who Do I Start.** He will only be used for that one week so choose who is the best available player at that position and add him. Do not fall in love with him as he will be axed (dropped) the next week, once your bye week/suspended player returns to action.

Long-term free agents (LTFA) are another matter. LTFAs will be on your team until they are hurt, benched or replaced by another LTFA. Therefore, there needs to be much more planning going into the decision to add them. Consider their injury history, the team they are playing for, the upcoming schedule, etc. **Use the rankings checklist in Chapter 6 for choosing LTFAs.**

There are three types of LTFAs. Starters, backups for the injured and sleepers or hunch players that you cannot afford to let sit on the waiver wire. Before grabbing a player from the waiver wire, ask yourself: why am I doing it? Why do I think he will perform now?

1) Look at past performance. If he failed to produce as a starter earlier and is playing only because the starter is injured, that does not necessarily make him a good starter.

2) Be conscious of opportunity; make sure he is going to play. There is no reason to pickup a QB, RB or WR who steps in for one week (while the starter is out) and has a career day, if that backup will never see the field again all season because the main starter is so good. Even if Jim Sorgi plays a great game and does well, do you really think Eli Manning is going to be benched? No, **opportunity is critical. Moreover, opportunity comes from the benching of the starter, a return from injury, or a trade.** Injuries to the starter also create opportunities but those are a little harder to predict. To realize the potential opportunities you need to do long-term thinking, not short-term planning. He is a low risk/high reward player, so add him one week earlier than other owners. He is an expensive risk the next week. Do not forget contractual issues. If a team has drafted or traded for a player high enough, they will want to see him on the field.

3) Supporting players are an integral part of a player's game. RBs need good OLs; QBs need good OLs, WRs or TEs to catch the ball; WRs need good QBs throwing to them.

4) Look for players dropped by other owners too early. Is the player in a slump, but is consistent year in and year out? Regression to the mean will dictate that he should put up better numbers the rest of the season. Is it a RB who just faced three of the top 10 rushing defenses? If so, grab him. One owner's trash is another owner's treasure.

5) Get players who will benefit your team. If you have four stud WRs and another falls in your lap, ask yourself if there is

another player at another position that you need more. Perhaps you should get the stud WR and trade another one of your star WRs to get a better player at another position.

Actions in the Preseason

Look at the position battles (especially QB/RB/WR) at training camp. If a rookie has a chance to beat out a veteran at a skill position, grab the rookie (if available) BEFORE he is named a starter. In other words, be proactive and grab the player before he wins the job. At worst, you can drop him after week 1 when he does not start. At best you have gazumped (bamboozled) all the other owners and made a big splash in the FA market before the season starts. **Remember rookie RBs have the best chance to succeed of any rookies, if given the opportunity.**

Watch for injuries and be ready to grab their backup, even if only for a short time. This gives you potential trade bait, HC material for the other owner whose player is hurt. Do not forget to remind him that his player is hurt now and may have problems all year with the nagging injury, so he needs his HC. It also blocks that owner from replacing his injured player with that backup.

Actions in the first half of the Season

Do not do anything for a week or two unless forced to by significant injuries, player suspensions, retirement, etc. Some players will start slow. There is no reason to drop a 3rd round draft pick simply because he puts up a few goose eggs (zero points) against tough defenses. **If you drafted someone in the early or middle rounds, you should hold onto them and let them have time to develop.** Look at Muhsin Muhammad in 2004. He had 2 TDs in the first six games and 14 TDs in the last ten games, to finish with 16 TDs. Imagine if you dropped him after week 7 when he caught just three passes for 28 yards and no TDs. Do not overreact in the first few weeks. Do not be the owner who says, "DOH! I wish I had just stayed calm and not cut Muhammad too early." Week 4 means the first bye week; now you can start to evaluate your team.

Do not expect much change in NFL starters the first month of the season. Just as you should not bench your studs too hastily, coaches who have named starters want to give them a chance too.

Build a watch list (list of potential players for your team at each position that are available on the FA list) the first few weeks of the season and be ready to go after the first month.

Consider upgrading at kicker if yours is not in the Top 10 by week 5. Kickers are a dime a dozen and some will be in the Top 10 that were not drafted.

Actions after midseason

Look for rookies with pedigree (did well in college) who are behind an aging vet. The "win now" mentality of the NFL means rookies are more likely to get a shot on NFL teams out of the playoff hunt who are trying to develop new talent for the future. Look to teams with three or less wins after week 9. Now look at their schedule for weeks 10-13. What will their record be then? Those weak teams will experiment with their starting rosters.

Many leagues stop transactions (trades/waiver wire pickups and add/drops) once the fantasy playoffs begin or even a few weeks before the fantasy playoffs begin. If this is the case, you need to make some team adjustments before the deadline. If you ran with only one player at a position during the year (rotating and adding/dropping based on matchup) then you now need to get a starter to stick with and a backup in case the starter gets hurt. Also, get rid of any players you do not absolutely need as either insurance or starters, and add RB depth. In some years, nearly 50% of the RBs in week 16 may not be the ones from week 1. Why? Injuries, suspensions, trades, rest for playoffs, benching, coach's decision, etc. So, before the deadline, go with only two QBs not three, only five WR (if start three), two TEs, two Ks (in all cases, an extra player in case one gets hurt) and one or two defenses. This will leave some room for more RB sleepers.

After the bye weeks are finished, once you have your main RBs ready for the playoff run, think about taking out some insurance policies (HCs) on them. If their backups are not already taken (by you hopefully) then grab them as a FA pickup just in case. You may even be able to trade away some bench depth and improve another position to make room for the HC. As an example, you have three bench spots with two good RBs and a WR and you would hate to have to drop one (and expose him to a FA pickup by an opponent as well) in order to make room for your HC. Why not try to trade one of the RBs and the WR to another team for a much better WR? Yes, a two for one trade. If executed, you will have upgraded your WR position (or have a much better backup WR) and you can fill the missing bench spot with a HC RB.

Think about playoff matchups when evaluating FA pickups. Who will he face in weeks 14-16? Use this as a discriminator.

Free Agency Blocking Strategy

Blocking – This is a tactic in which you grab a free agent player your opponent needs even though you do not need him. A perfect example occurs when a player goes down with an injury. He hurts his hand the previous week and then on Wednesday is declared out for the upcoming week. Your opponent this week is the owner of that player. If he has not handcuffed the players backup, then you would be wise to the backup off the free agent list.

This is beneficial to you in many ways. First, the backup may prove to be a good RB to start this week based on his matchup. Secondly, the starter may be out for the rest of the season, in which case you just picked up another starting RB. Perhaps best of all, you have BLOCKED this week's opponent from picking up a serviceable RB. He will be cursing you when he sees that you have scooped up his backup even though you do not need him. This can prove to be a very successful strategy.

The same thing can happen even if you do not want the backup. Say, for example, that Eli Manning goes down for your opponent this week; perhaps Jim Sorgi does not appeal to you as a good QB to have regardless of the status of Eli Manning. In that case, you can still BLOCK your opponent by grabbing the best QB available on the free agent list. This prevents your opponent from getting the better backup, assuming he does not have a suitable backup on his bench. QB, RB and TE will usually be the positions for which this strategy works best. Other positions (WR and K) are too deep and defenses never have injuries that would force an entire defense to be unusable.

Ten Free Agent Tips

1) Always have a "watch list" of at least three players from each position that you would add if you had an injury. Use your rankings - adjusted for injuries, suspensions and opportunities. Think about it this way: "If I could keep two more players at each position, who would I draft?" Perhaps they are sleepers that you want to pick up if they start to perform. Keep up with who is available and who was just released. When another fantasy owner adds a player, check out who they dropped and evaluate them for potential. Many times these are players drafted who have just not performed lately. Add them to your team if there is a reason to expect a rebound or if they are better than the players that you have on your team. **The players that are dropped most often, when a good FA or waiver wire player becomes available, are K2 and DEF2. Always be on the lookout to add one of these kickers or defenses if they can help you.**

NOTE: Many websites will let you mark players as watch list; this makes it easy to monitor them as the season progresses and allows you to delete players that others have added.

2) Use the upcoming schedule for LTFAs. Do they have favorable matchups? If a QB, look for weak pass defenses on their schedule ahead. If RB, look for weak rush defenses and kickers – poor defenses in general. Kickers playing in a dome in Dec are an advantage. A favorable schedule for your DEF/ST would involve playing low scoring offenses, inexperienced QBs, etc.

3) **Lead, don't follow, in free agent transactions; plan for your bye weeks at least two weeks in advance.** Try to be one-step ahead of the other owners. They will be thinking one week ahead. If you are looking for a WR or K that has a good matchup in two weeks, you are much more likely to get him than if you wait until one week away and have to compete with every other owner who is also looking for a bye week replacement player for that position.

4) **Do not waste roster spots on an extra TE, K, or DEF unless the rules force you to do so.** If the rules state that you must carry a certain number of those positions (such as two each) then you have no choice. If the rules do not state how many of each position you must have on your roster, carry only 1 TE, 1 K and 1

DEF. HINT: Try to draft each of those players so that they all have a different bye week; (i.e. TE has bye on week 7, K on week 8, DEF on week 9); if at all possible, try to get later bye weeks versus earlier bye weeks. This will give you more time to figure out if they are any good before the bye week and perhaps an add/drop will be better than picking up a fill-in for that position. Why carry only one from each position? It frees up roster spots for sleeper picks in other, more critical, positions. Simply carrying only one at all three positions will free up three places for sleepers. Then, when the first of those players has his bye week (TE in week 7, in above example), you will need to make a decision to either cut the TE and get a better one off the FA list (hopefully who has already had his bye) or drop one of the sleeper picks who has not panned out and pick up a fill-in TE for this week only. (See STFA.)

5) Handcuff your RB if he starts to have minor injuries or if the head coach indicates a change may be forthcoming. You should handcuff him in the draft (as we discussed earlier), but if you did not do it then, definitely HC him if your starter begins to come up a little lame at times. Nagging little injuries late in the game can be an indicator of problems ahead. The head coach making statements like "Willie Parker is our man for now," may be an indication of things to change in the future. Read between the lines.

6) If looking for a bye week pickup, make sure he has a great matchup in the week you are going to use him. For example, you select Peyton Manning as your #1 QB and do not draft another QB due to Peyton's reputation for never missing a game. Peyton has his bye week in week 6 so you need to add a QB in week 4 (two weeks early; think ahead, beat the rest) that has a favorable matchup in week 6.

7) A starter's injury can be your ticket to the acquisition of a great player. Look for injuries and grab the backup to the injured player, especially if it is a starting RB. What about an injury to your player? Your preparedness will determine the champions from the pretenders. Do you have the HC? Do you have a backup RB #3 to fill in? Can you trade away some bench depth to recover? If you do not have the HC, grab him immediately if your starter is out. Some will hesitate and begin to over-analyze. "What if he does not start?" "What if he is not any good?" GRAB HIM NOW. If you wait,

someone else will grab him to block you. He will definitely do better than your injured player who is out. **If he does not start, then try to grab the person who did start or make other plans for next week. Having a plan (grab his backup) is better than no plan at all.**

Do not forget to look at the FA list for star players who are injured and are off the radar screen. Always keep in mind when they are scheduled to return. You may have to add them a week earlier to keep the other owners out. Remember to be cautious with them when returning from injuries, but many times a pickup in week 10 or 11 can turn into a jewel at playoff time.

8) Avoid one-week wonders. Some owners will add a RB or WR who has one great game (ex. a 100-yard game). Evaluate him but also look critically at his performance. Was he a first week wonder? Did he play because the star was injured and could not play? Is he a new player on the team and this was just the beginning? Is he a RB who had three carries for 101 yards but one of those carries was a fourth quarter dash for 93 yards as the game ended? Did most of his points come in garbage time? A wait and see attitude is better than dropping good players chasing long shots.

9) Analyze game history. You can usually use websites to sort players based on their stats. Look at FP scored, and then look at TDs and yardage. Look at catches for WR and carries for RB. A player with many catches/carries but few yards may mean less TDs down the road, but someone with lots of catches/carries and yards may be just around the corner from scoring on those big plays. Rookies who are getting more and more touches should be considered sleeper material. **The longer you go into the season, the more you will need to look at game-by-game performances**. As an example, it is week 10 and you are looking at a WR to replace an injured WR#2. A WR with four TDs, but all of them in week 2, is not as good as a WR with only three TDs, one each from the last 3 games. What have you done for me lately?

10) Carry two kickers starting in the middle of November. Get your spare kicker before the end of the free agency period, if there is an end. This makes sure you are covered in case of injury after the FA period ends. There is nothing worse than seeing your kicker pull a hamstring on a fake kick, only to be sidelined for the

next 2-3 weeks and your playoff-bound team becoming kicker-less. Another reason to do this is to have another choice when the bad weather starts to affect games. If your K1 is playing outdoors in a swirling snowstorm, with a K2 at least you have other options.

Free Agent Aquistion Budget (FAAB) Notes

Assuming you start with a $1,000 FAAB, expect to pay anywhere from $100-$300 for a week 1 new starter; $300-$700 is the typical range for a good pickup during the season. Rarely do owners spend over $800 (too much of the budget spent on one player). Most of the spending occurs in weeks 3-5 and then it decreases as the weeks go by until the last week before the transaction deadline, where it picks up, presumably because owners know that they can spend all their money then. There is no reason to save money. You may see up to $900 later in the season if a new starter emerges (that is a sure thing) due to a season-ending injury. That, of course, assumes the owner has that much FAAB left.

Summary

1) Do not assume your team is perfect after the draft. Look for weaknesses (bye weeks, injuries, weak players, etc.) and players available after the draft who can fix the weaknesses.
2) Why use free agency? To fill a need for an injured, suspeneded, demoted, or poor performing player that cannot be met through your own bench.
3) Look for opportunity in the form of injury, suspension or trade of a starter.
4) Rookie RBs have the best chance of any rookies for success.
5) Do not drop early or mid-round draft picks too early in the season unless they are out for the season.
6) K and DEF are the easiest to upgrade through free agency.
7) Have two kickers by week 10 or before the FA period ends.
8) Use the same rules for WDIS decisions when trying to find a short-term (one-week) replacment. Use the checklist for ranking players when looking for long-term free agents.

Chapter 11 How do I improve my Team through Trades?

You can control three of four things that win championships; your draft, your lineup decisions and your waiver wire/free agent transactions. All of these are fully within your control. The other aspect to winning, which you do not control completely, is trades. It involves another human being. That other person is what makes it so tricky. Some owners love to trade, some are afraid to trade and some tolerate it as a necessary evil to improve one's team. Many owners fear trades because they are afraid of losing. If the trade backfires, things could be worse than they were before.

Most owners will come out of the draft thinking they have had a good draft and a perfect team. There is little to be gained by trading then, unless a team has obvious flaws, such as both QBs on the same bye week. Even then the owner may want some time to see how things develop. Trades usually happen after week 3 and not before. Why? Week 4 is the first bye week and it takes a few weeks of frustrating performance before some owners give up the ship. Hardly anyone gives up on a player after week 1. If they do, let me know, I want to play in that league. Injuries can be another reason for trades and they tend to start to pile up after a few weeks. Look for some activity after week 3 due to bye weeks but most activity will occur from week 5 up until the trading deadline, if there is one. A dip in trades may occur just before the deadline because some owners give up on getting a deal done close to a deadline.

Trading is allowed in some leagues, while in others, it is forbidden. The high stakes leagues usually prohibit it in order to eliminate the possibility of collusion. Collusion is a conspiracy between two or more owners where they intentionally try to improve one team at the expense of another. This is illegal and ruins the fun and joy of playing FF.

In lesser stakes leagues ($100 or less), trading may be allowed. If allowed, trading can be a fun and interactive way of playing the game. Some say that trading spices things up. One thing is for sure, more arguments come from trades than any other issue.

Trades that are unfair or bad (or perceived to be) can create bad feelings among the owners and toward the commissioner. They can cause teams to quit trying or drop out of the league altogether. **Avoid leagues that allow trades.** Trades are a hassle and a beginner has more chance of getting swindled.

There is an old saying in fantasy football, "Better no trade, than a bad trade." Make sure any trade you make benefits your team. Do not accept a trade just to be trading. You can go the entire season without trading. You can offer, counter-offer, accept or reject trades. No one is forcing you to do any of these. No reply after a certain time should be a rejection of a trade. Nevertheless, be respectful and reply to all trade offers. You do not have to accept a trade.

So why trade? Because the chances are high that at some point in the season your team will be affected by injuries, NFL coaching start/bench decisions, other players playing better or your players playing poorly. All of these can lead your team to be deficient in one area or another. Bye weeks also may force you to trade and the need to make a playoff push may nudge a trade here and there.

Trades can be good, bad, stupid or unfair. Ultimately, you are the one who pulls the trigger on the trade. **If you have to ask if you won or lost, you probably lost because you do not know why you made the trade; make trades that benefit your team.** You need to know how and why they will benefit you. **There are three reasons to trade: build depth (get a better RB#3 to cover RB1 or 2 on a bye week), improve a starter (QB#1 is now much better) or buy insurance (HC RB#1) to improve your deficiencies.**

Trades are more likely to occur in leagues with large rosters and less likely to happen in leagues with smaller roster sizes. Leagues with smaller rosters have more players available via free agency. Many times in a league with a small roster size, the other owner will want a little something extra to get the deal done. With a smaller pool of players on your team, it is hard to create something as a little extra. Often the only way to get the trade done is to give too much. Therefore, it is either a deal that is costly or no deal at all. In leagues with large rosters (typically dynasty leagues), owners have future draft picks, young up-and-coming stars and rookies with potential, all of which can help make a deal. **The more options you have to offer, the easier it is to get a trade done.**

Trading is a game of give and take. Think of trading like being a used car salesperson. You do not want to tell the other person exactly why you want to trade (or what the car's condition really is) because that may scare him away. On the other hand, you need to be as honest as possible so that he does business with you again or at least does not tarnish your reputation with other owners (customers). RBs will always be a desired trading commodity simply because of the law of supply and demand. You will rarely have problems getting takers for a trade involving a RB. The key is to make it worth it for you and the other owner.

Some terms before we proceed:

Proposed Trade – a trade that has been offered to another owner for acceptance. The owner considering it can accept, reject or counter-offer.

Accepted Trade – a trade that has been agreed to by two or more owners and that has been put to the league for approval.

Approved trade – a trade that has been approved by the league as official. Usually approval is given by the commissioner, a vote by owners or by no protest from a set amount of owners.

Types of Trades

1) Players at same position – You trade a RB to Team A and he trades you a RB back. Hopefully both players are of similar value. Then why trade? Maybe one owner likes the other RB better because he is on his favorite team or comes from his alma mater. Perhaps one of the players is on the same bye week as his other RBs. Perhaps one has a weak playoff schedule or a strong remaining schedule, etc.

2) Multiple player deal – this involves trading multiple players from each team. Usually it will involve one big player from each team. In other words, the player you have to move off your roster anyway, to make room for the main player, can be packaged as part of the trade. For example, you want to upgrade at TE and you have lots of WR depth. You offer Anquan Boldin (WR, Baltimore Ravens) for Antonio Gates (TE, San Diego Chargers).

You also offer to give Team A your TE1, Heath Miller (TE, Pittsburgh Steelers), for one of his WRs, Donnie Avery (WR, St. Louis Rams), who looks promising in the FF playoffs. You get two players, a TE and WR and he gets two players, a TE and WR. You both improve your teams by filling needs.

Trade Partners

There are five types of traders

    1) The ones looking to swindle

    2) Those looking to trade only if they get the clear upper hand in some way. For example, owners trying to get rid of someone whom they are going to drop in 2-3 weeks anyway; in many cases they are rarely willing to give away good for good.

    3) Those who like to talk trades but never go through with them.

    4) Suckers – those who will accept any trade

    5) Those looking to give and get fairly

    Get to know the other owners' tendencies in your league. Give them what they want, not necessarily what is good for them.

    Focus on owners who want to trade. Do not waste your time or energy with owners who have anti-trading tendencies as noted above. **Anytime you find teams with two good players but who can only start one you have a possible trading partner.**

Steps to execute a trade

    1) Identify what you need (your weaknesses). You are weak at TE. You have two of the league's worst and every time you add/drop one, he turns into a stinker too.

    2) Identify what you have to offer (your strengths). Your team's strength may lie in the fact that you have four starting RBs and can only start two per week (no flex). You can need three starting RBs (one for injuries, bye weeks and weak matchups) so you have an extra starting RB to trade.

    3) Look for what you need from other owners' teams. Determine which players in the league, on other teams, will fix your weakness. Have the names ready. You must have some objective in order to know when to proceed. Do not have just one name. "I

must have Antonio Gates," is not a need but a want. "I need a top three TE" is a much better objective.

4) Determine what the other owner needs.

5) Make an offer, utilizing your own personal strengths and weaknesses in the trade.

Trade Dos (Steps to a successful trade)

1) Compromise or overcome objections when they do not hurt your team. Sometimes a kicker or defense can sweeten the deal enough to get it approved. However, avoid too much compromise. Do not be so wrapped up in getting a trade done that you lose sight of the objective. **Compromising too much just to get a trade done is the worst thing you can do.**

2) Try to make the trade look like the other owner's idea. If you can get him to suggest the trade, you have a higher chance of getting the deal done.

3) State the obvious. Imply everything else. Minimize talking about why a trade is needed. In trades, less talk is more if you can get the other owner to jump to conclusions.

4) Use the "us versus them" mentality to build allies. This is especially helpful in leagues with divisions or where one team has dominated for several years. Try to build up a rapport with other teams in the other division that are fighting a "bully" or dominating team. When trading with an owner from another division, a simple "You need this to beat Team A this year. Do it and I will see you in the Super Bowl," can work miracles.

5) **Avoid trading with division rivals that can beat you for a title or playoff spot.** Trading with them after you have played them and have a comfortable lead over them is acceptable, especially if they have yet to play your division rival. In that case, the words of the ancient proverb, "The enemy of my enemy is my friend", would apply.

Trade Don'ts (Steps to an unsuccessful trade)

1) Don't congratulate the other owner on the trade. This will naturally make him suspicious of why you are so smug at making the trade.

2) Don't gloat or rub a trade in the face of anyone.

3) Don't get personal or emotional. Never attack an owner's intelligence, personality or family. If you have to walk away, then do so; but do it with dignity. Always say, "Thanks for the offer but I am going to decline. Maybe we can come to something next time."

4) Do not make a trade offer without looking at the other owner's roster. You look foolish offering to trade a RB to a team that has RB as their strength.

5) Never try to trade an injured or demoted player. If you want to move him, let the other owner know the player's situation; doing this one time will ruin any reputation you had as a fair trader.

6) Do not lie or make up stats or quotes. This will lead to other owners finding out and quickly labeling you as untrustworthy. However, if you state that Ryan Grant (RB, Green Bay Packers) is on track to score 14 TDs, after he has scored 7 by the mid- way point; that is a valid tactic. The fact that Green Bay played the easiest schedule in the first half of the season is something the other owner should evaluate. Statistics do not lie; other's interpretations of statistics is where the lying comes in. Remember Mark Twain – "There are lies, damned lies and statistics."

7) Do not assume that your trading partners rank players the same as you. If you think Ronnie Brown is worth more than Brian Westbrook, try to get a straight up trade. Do not sweeten the deal until asked. **Always start with your lowest (though not insulting) offer.**

Trade Communication

Communication is the key for any sucessful trade. Always keep the lines of communication open. Start with an innocent "What would it take to get Reggie Wayne (WR, IND)?" Even if the other owner says, "Nothing on your team," now you have established some communications and can go from there. **Always ask the selling price first, it may surprise you at how low it really is.** If you start with an offer, you may pay too much. Start out by asking "How much?"

Responses to Trade Offers

Always respond to offers in a timely manner. Nothing turns off an owner more quickly than no response to a trade offer. I hate having my offers just hanging in the wind while the rest of the league moves rapidly forward. If you only check the website twice a week, tell everyone. If you are going on vacation for a week, tell everyone so they will know you cannot communicate in a timely manner.

Some owners start low and like the art of haggling. Anyone who has been to the markets and bazaars of many European or Middle Eastern countries can relate to this tactic. They expect you to bargain and hope you will accept less than they are willing to part with. Counter their lopsided offer with your own reasonable offer (but not your best offer or that will remove some of your own wiggle room). Play their game but with less movement of positions. An offer of trade (even a bad one) is better than no offer at all. At the very least, you get to see who the other owner likes or values on your team and you have opened up some communications with them.

If the trade is totally unacceptable, explain why and move on. Nevertheless, be diplomatic in your explanation why a trade is not right for your team. **Trades are like some people's babies, owners and parents take great offense when their "children" are put in a bad light**. My worst reply is "Would you accept this trade if you were in my shoes?"

Seven Rules of Trading

1) Select trading partners based on need and personality. Look at all the rosters in your league and identify who is strongest where your need is. Now look at those teams and determine where their needs are. A great trading partner is strong where you are weak and weak where you are strong. It is a match made in heaven. You can help him and, for this, he will help you. Do not forget personality either. Remember the trading types. Never give up on any one owner but also do not waste too much time or energy on an owner that obviously does not or will not trade. **Many times new owners (beginners) will make friends with a few owners, develop close ties to them, and subsequently trade exclusively with them**. This is natural; people we know and trust are more likely to become trading partners. Just do not eliminate the other owners simply because you do not know them as well. Always have the trading door open.

2) Criticize in private, praise in public. My dad always told me that and it applies to the players on your team too. Never communicate your displeasure with a player openly. That just allows other owners to know how you feel and gives them the chance to lowball you during future trade negotiations about that player. If you have any criticisms, keep it private. Do not talk bad about your own players. On the other hand, always pump up and promote your players. Use stats to brag about them or use other's "expert" commentary. Other owners will soon covet your players and trade offers will come flooding in when others realize what great players you have.

3) Always do your homework. How will this trade affect my team? How will it affect the other owners team? What does his remaining Strength of Schedule (SOS) look like? What is his fantasy playoff schedule? What is the NFL players team doing? What is the status of his injuries or his teammate's injuries? Is there any competition for his job?

4) Know your deal breaker. You will not trade these players. Better to know these upfront and maybe even announce them to the other owner as "off the table." No reason to waste time with offers for them.

5) Present your case. If the trade really is win-win, you may have to sell his "win" portion. This could be because he does not see that he has a weakness at a certain position. Point out this flaw to him (diplomatically, of course) so that he can identify his needs.

6) Once the trade is a done deal; forget it ever happened and move on. No reason to gloat that you got a great deal. No reason to treat that owner more favorably in the future just because you got a trade accomplished with him. Do not rue the fact that you did not get everything you wanted. Now focus back on your team and continue to seek out strengths and weaknesses.

7) Establish relationships. Get to know ALL of the other owners. Ask them questions about their lives, philosophies and successes. Once you know the other owners, you can begin to get a better feel on how to handle trade negotiations with them.

Important Trade Tip

Here is some very simple but often unheeded advice: **Watch out for bye weeks coming up and account for them in player value.** Player A and B are equal in value. Player A has had his bye week, player B has his bye week coming up. Who would be the most valuable? Player A since he has all the games remaining as an asset whereas player B will miss one week of the remaining games due to his bye week. Also look at upcoming scheduled matchups and FF playoff matchups for your players and potential NFL players you could get from a trade.

Evaluating Trades

The best evaluation is to ask yourself: "Would I accept this trade if I was in the other owners shoes?"

Players involved, number of teams in the league, scoring system and rules involved all determine trade value. The number of teams will determine position demand.

Mathematical method of evaluating trades

One of the best methods is to use a trade (draft pick) chart (See _Fantasy Football Guidebook_ Appendix C Trade Analyzer). If you are offered the 5'th best player in the league for the 15th and 25th best players in the league, that is pretty much equal. The 5th overall pick of the draft is comparable to both the 15th and 25th picks. Try to put the players in terms of overall player worth and compare them as if they were draft picks

Trades can be good, bad, stupid or unfair.

1) Good trades are win-win situations. Good trades occur when both owners get something they need, thus improving their teams. Many times the ultimate trade winner or loser will not be determined until the season is over. Anytime there is no loser, only a better winner that is a good trade. For example if my new WR2

did better than your new QB1, but your QB was better than no QB, that is good enough for both teams. You should strive for all win-win trades, that way the owner will keep coming back for trades. Who would you rather trade with? The owner who swindled you or the one who gave you a win-win trade?

      2) Bad Trade – The trade is not even but the owner on the losing side is doing so for a reason. Unlike a good trade, a bad trade involves one owner gaining an advantage player wise. He needs a QB since both of his are terrible. He trades away a <u>better</u> RB to get some QB production.

      3) Stupid Trade – Trade where one team gets a player that is far more valuable than he trades away. This is a trade where you, as the owner, would never execute the trade, but it does not involve collusion; it is simply a trade with an owner who is desperate or unknowing. The losing owner just is not smart enough to know it is a losing trade, he does not know how bad it is or he made it by mistake. In all three cases, he has not colluded with the other owner. Stupidity is no excuse. But in trades, it can be a reason.

      4) Unfair Trade – An unfair trade involves an obvious disparity in trade values and thus may suggest collusion. Collusion is a conspiracy between two or more teams where they intentionally try to improve one team at the expense of another. This is illegal and hurts the whole league. If you notice this-get out or work with the commissioner or other owners to prevent it.

Trading Draft Picks

      If you know that you have the 4th pick of the draft but do not really care for the three or four RBs that will be around at that point, then try to trade down and get a lower first round pick (say 9th when you will be picking a RB that you really wanted anyway) and then get a higher 2nd round pick (or even more if you can negotiate it and the league will allow it). The opposite is also true. Let us say you have the 10th pick of a 12-team league and you really do not like what will be left over at RB (based on mock drafts and your overall rankings) by the time your pick comes up. In this case, try to trade up for an earlier pick so that you can get "Mr. Dependable (a Top 5 RB)" no matter what the cost. Another advantage of a draft day trade of picks is the confusion it causes other owners. Now it makes the draft harder to track (who you have drafted or need) because you have changed a few of your pick positions. This alone is worth trading picks, especially if it gets you away from some of the tougher owners.

Trade Timing

Timing can be the trading deadline, the big game versus a rival, or any chance of making the playoffs. Being the first to realize an owner needs something (his RB1 is now out for the season) can be a form of timing too. Look for key events. An owner loses his star WR to an injury. Now your bench WR who is starting and making ESPN highlight reels looks good as trade bait. Did your opponent's RB just produce another goose egg in week 7; time to get him some help. Two weeks before the trade deadline look at who is in the hunt and who needs help to stay in the hunt. Sometimes these owners are so playoff-obsessed that they will make a desperate trade to secure that player needed for the playoff push. **Injuries and time of the season can determine trade likelihood.**

Take advantage of these critical times:

1) Loss of a starter – An owner loses his WR1; your WR3 can fill the void if packaged right and if the other owner panics enough.

2) Slow start – If an owner starts slow and loses a few games or sees poor performance from a good player, now is the time to strike a deal.

3) Owner has bye week blues – easiest and most likely reason to get a trade done. Players for the same position, all on a bye the same week, calls for drastic action. Start to use it to your advantage by preying on the weak during their bye weeks.

4) Trying to make the playoffs – Owners can get desperate in their attempts to make the playoffs. Anything can be offered.

Trade Disputes (Is it a fair trade?)

What is a fair trade? Trades are subjective and different owners see different advantages. As the old saying goes, "beauty is in the eye of the beholder." What is good to one owner may be bad to another and unfair to a third. Basically, a trade should improve both teams in some manner. Some believe that there is no such thing as an unfair trade (both owners agreed to it). In other words, they feel that no owner would intentionally collude thus all trades must be allowed. This is the "Mary Poppins" theory of trades. They will never veto a trade simply on the principle that all parties agreed to it. Other owners say most are okay but some trades are unfair and need to be vetoed.

Many times the ones protesting the loudest about a lopsided trade are dead wrong. It takes a long time to determine the winner and many times it is not the team everyone thought was getting a steal. When we try to evaluate a trade as fair or unfair, we run the risk of imposing our own opinions on other's trades. You need to evaluate it from their perspective, not your perspective, and perhaps giving owners the benefit of the doubt is best in all but the most obvious circumstances. What is fair to one owner may be unfair to others (that is why we have the draft; opinions differ). I have vetoed a few trades and regretted it every time after watching those players involved.

What can be done if the trade seems unfair? First, post a message stating your objections and asking both owners to explain why they think the trade is good for both teams. Both owners should easily be able to explain why it is a fair trade to them. One person's perception of fair is another's perception of bad. Secondly, if you still have doubts, protest or veto the trade, if able. Speaking of vetoing trades, I prefer that the commissioner be left out of the equation and only league owners vote. One owner (the commissioner) should NOT have the power to approve/veto a trade.

Summary

1) Avoid leagues that allow trades.
2) If you have to ask who won a trade, then it was not your team.
3) There are three reasons to trade: a) build depth b) improve starters c) get insurance in case of injury
4) The more options you have, the easier it is to trade. (The better your team, the easier it is to trade.)
5) Teams with depth (i.e. two good players at a position but can start only one) make good trading partners.
6) Remember bye weeks in trades. Two equal players - one with a bye week past and one with a bye week coming up are not equal.

Chapter 12 What Resources Should I Use?

There are four main sources of FF information: magazines, books, televison and the internet. FF magazines come out in the summer and are specifially written for the upcoming season. FF books are scarce, but more have popped up in the past few years. Most are mainly strategy-based and are for differing skill levels. Television and radio shows are the easiest to find and cost nothing (unless you buy SirusXm or Satellite TV just for the FF shows). These programs usually get started in August. Finally, the internet is always available and has FF content 365 days a year. Some of this content is free, but much of the good, consice information comes at a cost.

To pay or not to pay, that is the question. You can pay to subscribe to a site that will provide you with FF information that in many cases can be tailored to your league's specifics; or you can abstain from paying for information that is free on the internet and just do it all yourself. For those who search for information themselves, their argument is that it is all free somewhere; you just have to find it. Many of the websites that support leagues also have excellent tools, databases and injury updates.

If you are time-limited and decide to go it alone, I suggest you focus your in-season research later in the week, if transaction rules allow (i.e. not first come - first served on free agency, or when a roster has to be submitted by Friday night every week). It is best to check on injuries on Saturday night or even better on Sunday morning, when these decisions are more likely to be finalized. In addition, some of the start/bench analysis that you may use to influence your decisions comes out on Fridays. **I highly recommend ESPN, YAHOO, CBSSPORTSLINE and the NFL websites as good free sites**. Be careful though, as some of these now offer premium services for an annual fee.

I recommend every beginner purchase at least one FF magazine, one FF book (_Fantasy Football Almanac_) and a subscription to a FF service like _www.Footballguys.com_. I will

explain why Footballguys is such great value for your money later in this chapter.

Total cost will be about $40 but it will make your life so much easier and save you time as well. Once you have a season or two under your belt and can go a little more extensive with your own research then you can forgo the internet help if you want.

There are several reasons why you should purchase the *Fantasy Football Almanac* book? First, it comes out a few days after the NFL draft so it is one of, if not the first, publication after the NFL draft. It starts the FF season. Second, it is a book and thus will not be ruined if you have it at the beach or the pool or your child spills orange juice on it. Third,since it is a book, it lets you cut the umbilical cord to the internet/computer and get outside or spend some quality quiet time with the family - albeit reading about fantasy football! How great is that? Fourth, it is large print so you can read it easily. And finally, it does not have distracting advertisements with models in bikinis striking provocative poses, so anyone can enjoy it and males reading it will not get scolding looks from their significant others.

Get your information from a variety of different sources but do not get so many that you cannot check them all. You need to find reliable sources and ones that can condense the information and speculate what its impact will be. Once you have a few trusted resources, use them.

There are so many FF magazines, websites and TV programs today, how do you pick the right one? We will discuss that next. No matter what type of media you choose, make sure the resources you choose "show their work."

Fantasy Football Magazines

You can become addicted to buying every fantasy football magazine on the rack, in the search for more and better information. It starts in early July when the first magazines hit the store shelves. You rush out and get the first one, even though it is not your favorite. Then, a few weeks later, you get your favorite. The week after that, you are out shopping with your better half and see a better-looking magazine and you pick that one up too. Every week there seems to be a different, better and newer magazine that is a must-have. I counted 20 fantasy football magazines on a magazine rack recently. Before you know it, you have spent $100 and have ten magazines, one for every room in the house. Stop the madness. Focus on two magazines. Ok, if you want to buy both, fine but stop at these two, as they are the best out there. The winners are *Fantasy Football Index* and *Fantasy Football Pro Forecast*. Both are the oldest of the FF magazines and both provide the most bang for your buck. Remember: get atleast one of these magazines, get the annual *Fantasy Football Almanac* (published May 1st every year) and subscribe to a premium website such as www.Footballguys.com.

The most important thing about magazines: Remember they come out in early July, so they were published, at best, in early June. **They will not be current.** You need to update them for injuries and player trades, etc. So why bother? They are expensive these days, with most cover prices in the $7-$10 range. Why buy two magazines at $17 when you just told me they were outdated? Why not use that money to go with a great web service that provides information for $25 and is always current? Good question! Call me old-fashioned but I like to hold something tangible in my hand. I also like to have it on trips so I can read something when I am away from the computer. It just feels good to have a big magazine around. In addition, it makes you look more sociable. If you stay glued to the computer all the time, your spouse, children or significant other may think you are obsessive. Try to avoid this. Buy a magazine or two and *Fantasy Football Almanac*. Okay, so why *Fantasy Football Index* and/or *Fantasy Football Pro Forecast*?

It is better to pick a magazine that comes out in July but that updates itself via its own website or e-mail updates to registered purchasers of the magazine. Make sure the updates are often and go up until you draft. Both of these do that with excellent websites. With these magazines you will be armed with the latest and greatest before you head into that draft room.

Both magazines represent the best investment for your FF dollar. They have rookie reviews, coaching changes, strength of schedule analysis and lots of expert rankings, projections and mock drafts. **Look for my rankings in these magazines each year.**

There is always an article on draft strategy. I find this is the best way to keep up with current thinking on draft strategies. I do not always leap onboard the latest and greatest strategy, but I do like to know what others are thinking. These magazines offer lots of opinions, rankings and picks. There are also the usual team reviews, but they give offensive line reviews as well, which most magazines do not do. Auction values are addressed too. Very few magazines will even mention auction values. Stick with these two leaders in the FF industry and you cannot go wrong.

No matter what magazine you use, make sure it lists or ranks enough players at each position. For example, a 12-team league starting 3 WRs and a flex may need to draft 84 WRs (7 WRs per team) (See Appendix D). Any position at which you start only one player (TE, K and DEF) may need more than you think. Even though you are possibly only going to draft one from these positions, there may be other owners who are going to draft two (good on them) or three so... be ready with a ranking of at least two per team from each position, just in case. Team profiles are important in that they will give you insight into the coaching changes and off-season trades, which player has a hot rookie waiting on the sidelines to replace him, etc. Read all the team profiles, as they will help you build a picture of the divisions, and more importantly, the competition when it comes time to analyze the SOS. Depth charts are critical, but remember that they will be outdated. It is best to get them updated right before the draft so that you know who will play and who will be the backups.

Of course, a magazine must have the NFL regular season schedule, week by week, so that you can do your own SOS analysis. The schedule should also include bye weeks. The magazine must have last year's NFL stats broken down by position (with last three years, if possible). One article that some do not include is a list or discussion of players who have changed teams. **Watch for this information since generally you will want to avoid these players (at least for the first half of the season since it takes time to adjust to a new system).** Inevitably, there will be an article or two on sleeper, or bust, candidates. File this information away as good-to-know and compare it with what others are saying. If the same player is on every sleeper list, then you know his value will increase and he may not be that much of a sleeper. In that case, he becomes a high risk/low reward player because you are paying excessively for the chance that he does prove to be valuable this year.

Newspapers

What about newspapers? Everything they say is going to be on the internet for free. The only advantage a newspaper may have is if local reporters are close to the team or follow the team and report something. In this case, local newspapers are a great source for scoops. However, even this news should be reported on a blog somewhere. **Avoid newspapers because they are too time-consuming and you should rely on other people to dig through these pages for you.** This is exactly what you pay Footballguys.com to do.

TV and Radio

Do you want the good news or the bad news? The good news is that there is more fantasy football awareness in the television media than ever before. The bad news? It is mindless and very simple and should be ignored. Anything these days with "fantasy" in the title is 75% likely to be worthless to you. Instead of providing a quality fantasy football product, it is more likely to be a rehash of "pick Peyton Manning as your QB and Adrian Peterson as your RB."

So what good programs are there in TV land? ESPN's Countdown, which comes on at 11 a.m. EST on Sundays, gives you an extra hour of information before the other pregame shows. It also has Chris Mortensen with injury updates. If possible use this information to change/tweak your roster in the last few minutes before the kickoff.

As far as the noontime (EST) pre-game shows, I admit to being a FOX fan. I enjoy Terry Bradshaw's humor; he is a regular person. I find Fox presents just the right amount of critical information and gives me some good laughs. I really enjoy Howie Long's commentary as well. He is articulate and to the point. When

Howie talks, I listen. One last thing I like about FOX is Jay Glazer, the FOX NFL expert. He gets the scoop and you get it before your starters deadline. CBS also does a good pre-game show too. Either show will serve you well.

Things are different when the games kick off. Currently I like to watch the CBS games because they have a ticker with game stats that are great for fantasy football. It goes through each game and includes QB, RB, WR, K and DEF stats. What a great system. FOX has no such ticker. They even trick you into thinking they are doing a ticker, but then it just advertises their website. DOH! So to recap, try to watch the ESPN pre-game show from 11-Noon. Then Fox pre-game from 12-1PM and then whichever games you prefer or CBS if both FOX and CBS have good games.

NBC has the Sunday night games. ESPN does Monday Night Football. NFL Network entered the realm of broadcasting NFL games with their Thursday night games. However, you may need to have DirecTV satellite to watch the NFL network or go to a local sports bar like Buffalo Wild Wings.

There are also weekly shows that are great for giving you fantasy insights, even though they do not cater exclusively to fantasy footballers. NFL Live comes on weekdays at 4 p.m. EST on ESPN during the football season. Another reason to have cable or satellite TV. It provides 30 minutes of NFL news and commentary by Trey Wingo, Sean Salisbury and Mike Golic. **NFL Live is a must-see if you do not have the NFL Network**. It gets you caught up on everything that is happening around the league. "Inside the NFL" on HBO is a good recap of what happened the previous week. Before the NFL Network, it was the only thing on TV to review other than ESPN News. **Now with the NFL Network, I find that is my sole viewing choice.**

The best network for information in general has to be the NFL Network. To quote its own website: "It is every football fan's dream. Seven days a week, 24 hours a day, 365 days a year; a television network solely devoted to the most popular sport in America, professional football." YES! It is like the NFL on C-Span. They have all preseason games not shown on network TV and more access to players and coaches than anyone else. At any given moment, if you tune in, you will have the latest information from around the league. It is a must-have network on cable. They even have NFL Replay to see games you missed (if you do not have NFL Ticket). Moreover, they show Thursday and Saturday games exclusively on the network live. Then there is the Total Access program (M-F, 7 p.m.), which can be your sole source of everything NFL. It includes Adam Schefter, one of my favorites, as the NFL expert. He reported that Oakland Coach Art Shell would not be around in 2007 and Oakland called Schefter a rumormonger; Oakland fired Shell a few weeks later.

NFL Playbook on NFL Network is not a fantasy show, per se, but addresses many of our needs, including upcoming matchups, league developments and injuries. Remember this though, to get NFL Network and all the programs and Thursday NFL games, you need DirecTV. I do have one criticism of the NFL Network. When will the NFL Network wise up and add some real fantasy shows to their lineup? They show repeats often. Why not add a good hour long, twice weekly, FF show. It would gather a larger viewing audience than their reruns.

Radio

ESPN radio show Mike and Mike in the morning (6-10 a.m. EST). Co-hosts Mike Greenberg and Mike Golic. Great show.

Sirius XM has several shows including the Fantasy Football Show (Tues 7 p.m, Fri 8 p.m.), Tailgate Show (Sun 9 a.m.) and the Sunday Drive (Sun 12 Noon). In fact, they have a dedicated Fantasy Sports channel XM 241 or Sirius 125.

Internet

Premium (pay) websites provide information and analysis that save you time. Sure, you could bookmark a hundred sites and get injury updates, weather updates and coaching announcements, but it would take a lot of time to check them all out each week. These premium sites give you lots of information and analysis at the push of a button. Soak up their information like a sponge and use their analysis as a great second opinion. However, remember that you make the call, you have to make the decisions and you are responsible for all the glory and shame that goes with it.

Narrow your focus when considering websites. Seek out sites that are fantasy football only. Try to avoid sites that do multiple fantasy sports. How good can you be at football if you also do baseball, etc.? Also, be wary of the sites that say "fantasy sports" in their title. Too broad.

Whether you go premium or free, try to limit it to three so that you can check them regularly. Not included in those three are a separate weather site and an injury site to look at on Sundays. The three I referred to are primary information sites. One may be a pay site where you can get rankings, weather status, who do I start (WDIS) information, etc.; the other might be a free site where your local league is located, just to get the big picture and one could be a magazine site just for a different opinion. Look for sites that have everything you need and include e-mails with updates. Perhaps use Yahoo or CBSSPORTSLINE as a quick backup and either footballdiehards.com (that goes with the *Pro Football Fantasy Football* magazine) or the *Fantasy Football Index* website. Another free information source comes from message boards (MB). Join a MB and use it to network to find like-minded FFers.

If you want to go for a paid site one I recommend is www.FootballGuys.com. For a low annual subscription price ($26.95) you get everything you need including player injury status right up until kickoff. It includes depth charts, draft rankings, weekly projections, game time injury and weather news and free entry into money contests. One site with all the information you need. What could be simpler? www.FootballDiehards.com is another great website with tons of information and insightful analysis.

Find a magazine or website that has an e-mail list and sends out at least daily or weekly updates. Find one that sends out "breaking" news on the big players and even sends out their cheat sheet with injury status (P, Q, O) by the player's names, so you can be reminded of making lineup changes and know the latest information. All of this information is on www.Footballguys.com and www.FootballDiehards.com, which is why I recommend them.

What is the best free site? That will depend on your style and the information you seek. **NFL.com, ESPN.com and Yahoo.com are the best free sites.** The ESPN website has live draft info, FPs scored against, projections, added/dropped (to give you an idea of what others are doing in other leagues), injuries, etc. Some have criticized them as being too "cookie-cutter" and trying to bring everything into "their world." I think they do a good job for what they do. Yahoo and CBSSPORTLINE are also free and provide valuable information, if you know where to look. Some "internet shows" discuss fantasy football exclusively. Yahoo and ESPN both have these webcasts. NBC Sports has "Fantasy Fix" with Gregg Rosenthal and Tiffany Simons. Find one you like and use it regularly to keep up with events. (See Appendix C Resources for a list of some of these sites.) Broadband internet is the only way to go if you are going to rely on these sites for instant scoring updates and detailed last minute updates.

Finally, what can you get out of these resources? What should you take away from all these sites, TV shows and print devices? First, seek out expert rankings, preferably a consensus by a number of "experts." Use this as your basis for what the other owners may be using. You should take it and tweak it, to make it a far better resource, but first find a consensus expert ranking in one of the magazines floating around. If you do not have the time to create your own rankings (See Chapter 6 – Ranking Players) then use the best-preprinted cheat sheet you can find. Just make sure the scoring and starters/rosters are the same. Look at the mock drafts, they let you know where the tiers of talent are and where the huge drop offs occur. They also alert you to new players who may not have been discovered by your research. Before the season starts, make sure you find the offensive depth charts. These are invaluable to see who is starting or close to starting as far as HCs and up-and coming players.

Books

There are other books on the subject of FF. Here are a few that are in my library:

Fantasy Football Tips: 201 Ways to Win through Player Rankings, Cheat Sheets and Better Drafting - Sam Hendricks

Fantasy Football Guidebook: Your Comprehensive Guide to Playing Fantasy Football - Sam Hendricks

Fantasy Football Almanac (annual) - Sam Hendricks

Fantasy Football's Big 6 and *Drafting to Win*- Robert Zarzycki

Fantasy Football The Next Level-David Dorey

Your Official Guide on How to Dominate Fantasy Football-Randy Giminez

Committed: Confessions of a Fantasy Football Junkie-Mark St Amant

Why Fantasy Football Matters (And Our Lives Do Not)-Erik Barmack and M. Handelman

Fantasy Football for Dummies-Martin Signore

Fantasy Football for Blood and Profit-Pete Smits

The Winner's Guide to Drafting a Fantasy Football Team- Chris Lee

Brotherhood of the Pigskin: A Fantasy Football Novel-Wade Lindenberger and Mike Ford

Martin Signore does an excellent job covering Yahoo FF leagues in *Fantasy Football for Dummies*. Randy Giminez does an eqlly good job discussing CBSSportsline FF leagues in *Your Official Guide on How to Dominate Fantasy Football*. Both cover those formats in detail.

Summary

1) Purchase either or both *Fantasy Football Pro Forecast* or *Fantasy Football Index magazine*.

2) Purchase *Fantasy Football Almanac* as a great draft preparation book when it comes out after the NFL draft.

3) Subscribe to *www.Footballguys.com* website service.

4) Watch the pregame shows before the games.

5) Read some other books on FF.

Chapter 13 Is there anything else I should know?

I recommend beginners avoid some of the specialty leagues like auction drafts, IDP and keeper leagues. However if you wish to try them early in your FF career, you need to know a litle about them. _Fantasy Football Guidebook_ goes into much more detail including entire chapters on each. For a small glimpse at the advantages and disadvantages of each, read on.

Auction Drafts

Recent studies show that 95% of fantasy owners who have tried both the traditional and the auction draft methods prefer the auction method! That is a significant percentage. In my experience, I have not seen 95% of fantasy owners agree on anything. In fact, if someone was handing out free money at the post office, only 80% would agree it was a good idea to go to the post office. I have never heard of a league switching to auction format, not liking it and switching back to a traditional draft. Yet many leagues still rely on the traditional draft.

As a fantasy owner in a traditional draft, you cannot select NFL players that were drafted prior to your turn. Therefore, unless you are lucky enough to have the first pick of the draft, your favorite player may not be available to you when it is your turn to select. If you have the 10th pick in a 12-team league, you know you will have every NFL player to choose from except nine (the nine taken with the first round picks in front of you) and then with your second round pick you will have a choice of every NFL player minus 14 players. If you know your draft pick in advance, you can predict who will not be available in most cases. In an auction draft, however, ALL players in the NFL are available to you until someone outbids you. Your only limitation in an auction draft is the amount you are willing to "spend" on a particular player. If you bid the most from your salary cap "money" on a player, then he goes to your team. After each draft selection, your "salary cap" is reduced by the amount of "money" you "spent" on the player just drafted. This continues until all rosters are filled on each team. This way, each team has an equal chance of drafting any NFL player. It is the highest bidder who ultimately gets him.

There are many auction advantages; the biggest of which is the fact that draft position no longer matters. You will never miss a chance at a player unless you "cap out" by spending all of your cap money. Auctions are more fun because every few minutes a different player is up for auction and everyone can have a stake in what happens, versus waiting 30 minutes before the next pick comes back to you in a serpentine draft. Auctions also have more strategies; if you want to spend most of your money (70%) on two or three 1st round picks from a traditional draft, you can. On the other hand, if you do not want to risk big money on a bust, you can get more 2nd-4th round players from a traditional draft for less money. Alternatively, if you love the Minnesota Vikings (and who doesn't?), you can try to get ALL Vikes on your team. It is much easier in an auction than a traditional draft. If you want an all-star WRs team, you can have that. Any player you want is yours, as long as you can afford him.

There are many auction misperceptions. Entrenched owners who have never tried an auction will haul out these excuses occasionally. "Auctions are time-consuming." Well, not anymore than a traditional draft, if you stick to time limits. Auctions will go faster in the later rounds as owners run out of cash and cannot afford to bid. "Auctions are complicated." Only if you cannot add or subtract. The most famous refrain of all is, "But we have always drafted traditionally." I reply with "A traditional draft compensates those who have not done their homework." Why play in a league that rewards laziness? Instead, try a league that has as its mantra: "Any player you want, just not every player you want!"

IDP Leagues

There are opponents of the DEF/ST concept. They claim that DEF/ST is too basic. Sure, it is good for the casual fan since it requires little involvement (that is why I recommend it for beginners), but there is more luck involved. There is no consistency from year to year, and let's face it, most leagues draft defenses with the last picks, so DEFs are boring. If you want to expand your fantasy football playing experience and get more detailed in the defensive realm, then individual defensive players (IDPs) may be for you. With IDP you do not draft entire defensive teams but instead draft (as the name implies) individual defensive players. How many you draft is up to you. If the league wants to start slow, then maybe just draft one defensive player. Remember these IDPs will be replacing the points provided by your DEF/ST. Some leagues say any defensive player can be drafted; others specify certain positions within the defense. For example, defensive lineman (DL), linebackers (LB) and defensive backs (DB).

Most leagues will have between 3 and 6 IDPs. Many IDP leagues will allow you to draft the same amount of IDP players as offensive players. So in a typical 1 QB, 2 RB, 2 WR, 1 TE, 1K league, you will also have 7 IDPs consisting of 2 DL, 2 LB and 3 DBs. Allowing this many IDPs also forces the IDPs to be valued on par with offensive position players and thus prevents the drafting of all offensive players then IDPs as an afterthought. Think longer drafts!

Why use IDPs? Well if the purpose of fantasy football is to bring NFL football to you in a realistic manner, then picking your own defensive players (versus being handed an entire team with one draft pick) is more realistic. This sense of "ownership" at building your own "Purple People Eaters" is another reason why many IDP leagues are also keeper leagues. Individual defensive players enhance the sense of controlling your team's destiny from year to year and building a legacy. Once you have played IDP, you will not go back to a simple team defense. **IDP leagues are the PhDs of fantasy football.** They are slowly becoming more popular but to date, the majority of leagues are still team defense or no defense oriented. **The bottom line is you should try an IDP league later in your FF career to see if you like it or not.**

Keeper Leagues

Leagues can be classified as either redraft or keeper (also called holdover or rollover) in terms of ownership. In a redraft league, each year all owners start from scratch. No players from previous years are kept. In a keeper league, owners can "keep" or retain any number of players for the next season. The number of players, number of years they can be kept, and the exact circumstances are based on the league rules and can differ from league to league. Keeper leagues can be further broken down by the number of players that can be kept. If a league keeps less than half of the players from the previous year (in order to prevent one team from becoming too dominant), then it is referred to as simply a keeper league. The less players that can be kept, the more a keeper league resembles a re-draft league However, if more than half of the roster is kept (including in many cases all of the roster) then that league is called a dynasty league.

Some of the advantages are:

1) It can help to individualize a team more. "Oh yeah, that's the Vince Young team;" since Vince was drafted in 2006 and held for several seasons, thus illustrating the owner's great vision.

2) It can help bring owners back for the next season since they have a connection to their team and the league (versus an entire re-draft each year or a complete do-over).

3) A good draft (especially the first one) can benefit you for many years.

4) You can "grow" younger players and watch them develop and reward your team.

5) You have the ability to plan for the future (next season) by trading good veterans this year for younger players or draft picks next year.

6) It is more realistic (mirrors the NFL) than a redraft league.

7) It encourages more participation even if you are out of the running for the playoffs because you can build for next year through free agency and trades.

8) Allows the owners to stay involved in the off-season because they have to make decisions on which players to keep, if any, before next year's draft. So they will track others' players and possible keepers and have to factor that into the draft (less supply, more demand).

Some point out that keeper leagues might have a weakened draft in future years, and consider it a disadvantage. After the inaugural draft, the other drafts are not as fun; since there will be fewer players to draft from, so it is less of an experience. This is particularly true in dynasty leagues where future drafts are just rookies or dis-carded players. However, in keeper leagues where only a small number can be kept, the drafts are just as fun but with more strategy.

In general, keeper leagues provide more of the real feel of managing a team. They also add to the enjoyment of fantasy football. Minimal (or partial) keeper leagues are the best of both worlds. By minimizing the number of keepers to one or two players, you still get the same competitiveness of trying to find a real sleeper for the next year, but you maintain your league's integrity and fullness of the draft year in and year out. Only allowing players picked after the early rounds to be keepers assures that the perennial great players (studs) are not kept and ensures that true sleepers will be tried.

Playoff Strategies

The following are two tips on how to maximize your chance to win in the playoffs.

1)   Play the best matchups. Do not be afraid to sit someone you have started all year long if they have not produced down the stretch. There is no reason to be loyal to the first RB you drafted back in August if he does not have the juice or the matchup to help you win.

2)   Do not take unnecessary risk. Look at your opponent. What has he scored the last few weeks? What is his weekly average? Moreover, what is your weekly average? Are you going to need a big day or can you coast and make him try to do something big? Do not take a risk on a boom or bust player now, unless you feel you need it to have any chance of winning. If your team has consistently outscored his, do not take any chances. Stick with the reliable fantasy point (FP) providers you have. If you are playing a team with Adrian Peterson (RB, MIN) and you have no way of winning unless you come up big, then and only then, look for some pickups to help.

Becoming a Commissioner?

Starting your own league can be just as fun as joining an existing one. By starting from scratch, you can set the rules the way you think they should be (See Chapter 3 Where do I start). If you are the commissioner, you can make sure your owners are the kind of people you want to play against and you can determine what is, if any, the prize structure. And last, but not least, if you are the commissioner you know the work will get done and done right. If you want more ideas on how to be a commissioner, see *Fantasy Football Guidebook*, Chapter 19 Commissioner Information.

Final Tips for a Beginner

Finally, here are some tips for the beginner. First, some fantasy football etiquette or "how to behave in your first league." Although these are not official rules of protocol, you cannot go too far off by following them. It makes for a more enjoyable experience for everyone involved. You may find that if you can find enough other owners to follow these 15 rules of etiquette you will have the perfect league.

FF Etiquette

1) Know the rules before you agree to join a league. There are few things worse than an owner who constantly asks questions or make "mistakes" about the rules when they are clearly posted.
2) Don't play in too many leagues - this is known as TMTS (too many teams syndrome). As a beginner, just play in one league and give it your all.
3) Make sure everyone in the league has your full name, phone number and email address.
4) Don't complain about your draft spot - suck it up and move on.
5) Pay your entry fee on time.
6) Arrive to the draft on time.
7) Keep up with who has been drafted and who is out for the season.
8) Don't threaten to quit if you do not get your way.

9) Don't forget to turn in a competitive roster every week - i.e. check for byes, injuries, suspensions, etc. No one wants their other league mates to play an opponent with empty roster spots.

10) It goes without saying that you should never cheat - I do not mean by following the rules - I am all for that. I mean by colluding with another team to cheat - like a lopsided trade or to block a beneficial trade simply because you do not like the other owner.

11) Never quit on a team. Even though you may be out of the playoffs, you still need to try to improve your team as if you were in the playoffs.

12) Don't bug other owners with tons of trades. Let it happen naturally.

13) Respond to trade offers in a timely manner.

14) Smack talk is fine, as is trash talking, but do not let it get personal. Foul-mouthed insults (bringing someone else's family heritage into the discussion) is taboo. Usually the trash talking is conducted via message board or email. Tip: Let the sun go down before you reply to a negative post. It always looks a little less confrontational in the morning. Give the other owner the benefit of the doubt.

15) Win, or lose, with class.

Top 10 Tips to Success for Beginners

1. Know all of your league rules. This includes scoring, starters, rosters, free agency, trades and tiebreakers.

2. Do not drink and draft (or set lineups while intoxicated).

3. Have a plan for the draft.

4. Know who is hurt, suspended, fired, retired or holding out and who has been drafted already during the draft.

5. Always set a legal lineup each week. This means replacing bye week players and those too injured to play.

6. Try to improve your team during the season using free agency or trades if allowed.

7. Get help - use a premium (pay) web site.

8. Watch the pre-game shows for news about players. If you cannot watch all the games, then at least watch the first games at 1 PM (EST) since the majority of teams play then.

9. Trust no one in your league for advice on who to start, trade, or add/drop.

10. Make your own choices. Trust your gut.

Top 10 Mistakes for Beginners to Avoid

1. Drafting a QB too early (1st round)
2. Drafting a K or Def/ST before your RB and WR backups
3. Relying too much on rookies
4. Thinking draft went perfect and then not checking the waiver wire or free agency list for potential missed players
5. Not having a balanced team
6. Benching great players (studs) simply because they face a tough defense or have a bad game
7. Dropping good players after two weeks of poor performance
8. Over analyzing the "who do I start" decisions
9. Becoming caught in a run on positions in the draft
10. Lopsided trades

Final Thoughts

Easy strategies or tips are just that - easy. There is a reason they are so easy. They have been simplified and generalized to make them easy to understand. They will probably work 80% of the time. Taking the easy path does not mean you will win a championship. It means you will be competitive, that is all. The easy way does not work all the time and may skip other accepted winning ways simply because they are hard to implement.

The hard way is complicated, takes more time and effort and will be more comprehensive. The hard methods provide that extra 20% of productivity, but require 80% more work. Is it worth it? If you want a better chance of winning consistently, it is worth it.

As a beginner, the easy way will introduce you to FF and give you a fighting chance of doing well. But if you want to win consistently, you will need to work harder. Remember, you are playing to have fun. If you are not enjoying your FF experience, you are doing it wrong.

Appendix A Supply and Demand Table

Pos	NFL	FF (4)	8 Team	10 Team	12 Team	14 Team	16 Team
QB	32	2	16(50%)	20(63%)	24(75%)	28(88%)	32(100%)
RB	46	3	24(52%)	30(65%)	36(78%)	42(91%)	48(104%)
(5)	(1)	4	32(70%)	40(87%)	48(104%)	56(122%)	64(139%)
WR	70	4	32(46%)	40(57%)	48(69%)	56(80%)	64(91%)
	(2)	5	40(57%)	50(71%)	60(86%)	70(100%)	80(114%)
TE	32	2	16(50%)	20(63%)	24(75%)	28(88%)	32(100%)
K	32	2	16(50%)	20(63%)	24(75%)	28(88%)	32(100%)
DEF	32	2	16(50%)	20(63%)	24(75%)	28(88%)	32(100%)
DL	124 (3)	4	32(26%)	40(32%)	48(39%)	56(45%)	64(52%)
LB	100 (3)	5	40(40%)	50(50%)	60(60%)	70(70%)	80(80%)
DB	128	4	32(25%)	40(31%)	48(37%)	56(44%)	64(50%)

Notes:
1) 1 primary RB per team plus 14 RBBC teams
2) 2 WRs per team plus 6 WR3's who are good enough to start
3) Based on teams using 3-4 and 4-3
4) 2 RBs +3 WRs as starters plus a backup at each position is the top number. The bottom number is based on leagues with 2 RBs +3 WRs, and 1 Flex position and one backup.
5) These numbers can be misleading because the rise of RBBC on teams increases RB supply but dilutes their performance

Appendix B Cheat Sheet Sample-QB

Adj	Rank	Player	Team	Bye	Notes
	1	Peyton Manning	IND	6	Never missed game
Up	2	Drew Brees	NO	5	No RB
	3	Aaron Rodgers	GB	5	Good OL
?	4	Tom Brady	NE	8	Avg 09'
		End Tier 1			
++	5	Phillip Rivers	SD	5	
Up	6	Donovan McNabb	WAS	4	New Team
	7	Tony Romo	DAL	6	
Up	8	Matt Schaub	HOU	8	2 good WRs
		End Tier 2			
Dn	9	Jay Cutler	CHI	5	New Scheme

Appendix C Resources

Free Games
www.yahoo.com
www.cbssportsline.com
www.espn.com
www.NFL.com

Premium Sites
www.Footballguys.com
www.Footballdiehards.com
www.bfdfantasy.com

FF Magazines
www.Fantasyindex.com
www.fspnet.com

Pay Leagues
www.theFFPC.com
www.wcoff.com
www.fantasyfootballchampionship.com

Other good sites
http://www.NFL.com/injuries
http://pro-football-reference.com
www.TWC.com
www.FFGuidebook.com

Appendix D Typical 12-team League Information

Assumptions: H2H, redraft, 18 man roster, start 1 QB, 2 RBs, 3 WRs, 1 TE, 1 K and 1 DEF/ST, FA waiver wire, no trades, no min/max on positions in draft.

Scoring rules: 4 Pass TD, 6 other TDs, 1 pt/20 pass yards, 1 pt/10 rushing or receiving yards. 1 PPR.

Expect the typical roster to include: 2.3 QBs, 5.2 RBs, 5.7 WRs, 1.8 TEs, 1.5 Ks and 1.5 DEF/ST

Rank 30 QBs, 70 RBs, 80 WRs, 25 TEs, 25 Ks and 25 DEFs for draft.

Draft plan: Get 2 QBs, 6 RBs, 6 WRs, 2 TE, 1 K and 1 DEF/ST or a safer mix would be 2/4/6/2/2/2.

Expected positions to be drafted per round
Rd 1: 10 RBs, 2 WRs (1.07 and 1.09)
Rd 2: 2 QBs, 4 RBs, 6 WRs
Rd 3: 2 QBs, 5 RBs, 4 WRs, 1 TE
Rd 4: 2 QBs, 4 RBs, 5 WRs, 1 TE
Rd 5: 1 QB, 2 RBs, 8 WRs, 1 TE (at this point 25 RBs and 25 WRs have been drafted)

Rough equivalents between positions
QB5=RB20=WR16=TE2
QB8=RB26=WR24=TE3
QB14=RB31=WR35=TE11

Expected player fantasy points based on the above league.
Note the break points - these are the tiers at positions.

QB 1-3   360 pts
QB 4-10   315

QB 11-18   260
QB 19-21   205
QB 22-25   175

RB 1   370
RB 2-4   320
RB 5-10   245
RB 11-20   200
RB 21-25   175
RB 26-30   160

WR 1-6   285
WR 7-10   255
WR 11-16   235
WR 17-21   205
WR 22-32   175
A slow gradual decline from WR 33 downwards

TE 1-3   285
TE 4-8   235
TE 9-14   170
TE 15-19   140

K 1-2   155
K 3-12   130
K 13-27   100

DEF 1-3   175
DEF 4-7   155
DEF 8-21   130 (DEF 22-27   110)

Typical team scores are in the following range:

Great score   145
Good score   135
Average Score   120
Poor Score   105
Terrible Score below 100

Appendix E Easy Draft Plan

Assumes a 12-team league with 18 man roster, starting 1 QB, 2 RBs, 3 WRs, 1 TE, 1 K and 1 DEF/ST

Rd	Position Seeking	Notes	Comments
1	RB	Top 10 RB	If later draft spot (11th or 12th), may not get Top 10 RB, go top WR and then get RB with 2nd pick.
2	WR	Top 10 WR	If you drafted early in the 1st, may not get a great WR here
3	QB	Top 5 QB	After this pick you can wait on QB2
4	TE	Top 5 TE	Now you can wait on TE2 till late
5	RB or WR	RB	Best available RB or WR (RB 90%)
6	Other position	WR	If picked RB last round get WR this round
7	WR		He will start so get best WR here
8	RB		Should have 1 QB/3 RBs/3 WRs and 1 TE by now
9	WR	WR4	Backup for your 3 WRs byes
10	RB	RB4	Handcuff your RB1 backup
11	WR	WR5	
12	RB	Sleeper	If need 2 K+DEF. get QB2 here
13	WR	Sleeper	If need 2 K+DEF. get TE2 here
14	QB2		If need 2 DEF, get first DEF here
15	TE2		If need 2 Ks, then get first here.
16	DEF/ST	DEF1	
17	K	K1	Not on bye with DEF1
18	?		Clean up problems with this player

Appendix F Hard Draft Plan

Assumes a 12-team league with 18 man roster, starting 1 QB, 2 RBs, 3 WRs, 1 TE, 1 K and 1 DEF/ST

Rd	Position Seeking	Notes	Comments
1	RB		Top 10 RB
2	WR		Top 5 WR unless drafted early in 1st
3	RB		Can always go WR if better value
4	WR		Must have 2 RBs and 2 WRs
5	RB		Can always go WR if better value
6	WR		Must have 3 RBs and 3 WRs
7	WR		Should have 3 RBs and 4 WRs
8	QB	QB1	Wait til 8th rd or later and get a QB ranked 10th-12th
9	TE	TE1	Try for the last of the Top 12 TEs
10	QB	QB2	Best available QB
11	TE	TE2	Best available TE
12	RB	RB4	Handcuff RB1 backup
13	WR	WR5	
14	RB	Sleeper	If need 2 DEF, get first DEF here
15	WR	Sleeper	If need 2 Ks, then get first here.
16	DEF/ST	DEF1	
17	K	K1	Not on bye with DEF1
18	?		Clean up problems with this player

Appendix G Breakout WR Checklist

(2010 as an example below in bold)

1) Take the top 2 WRs from each team that had a Top 15 QB last year (2 x 15=30). **NFL teams from 2009 were GB, NO, IND, HOU, NE, SD, DAL, MIN, PIT, NYG, AZ, PHI, CHI, JAX, CIN**

2) Eliminate some teams because last year was a fluke. They may have played a very easy schedule or their Top 15 QB may have left the team. If this was the case, remove those WRs. With this discriminator, you will lose an average of six WRs. (30-6 players =24 WRs). **For 2010 MIN, PIT, AZ and PHI are eliminated. So 30-8=22 GB, NO, IND, HOU, NE, SD, DAL, NYG, CHI, JAX, CIN**

3) Remove any WRs on this list who were in the Top 15 WRs last year. Everyone knows about them and they will be ranked high. 24-15=9. **In 2010, 8 of the top 15 WRs came from the remaining teams above. Therefore, our list is now 22-8=14.**

4) Of the remaining WRs, the ones in their 2nd-5th season are your candidates. The more experienced they are (5th year being the most experienced), the higher they should be ranked. This usually results in 6-8 breakout WR candidates.

For 2010, it predicts the following:

Devin Hester	**CHI**
Austin Collie	**IND**
Mike Sims-Walker	**JAX**
Robert Meachem	**IND**
Hakeem Nicks	**NYG**
Julian Edelman	**NE**

Appendix H Who Do I start (WDIS) Checklist

The order of these steps is important. Later steps should generally not override earlier steps.

Rule #1 – Always set a lineup; (remember early week Thursday and Saturday games)

Rule #2 – Always begin this WDIS process with your top picks from the draft

Rule #3 – Always start your studs

Rule #4 – Never start a player on a bye

Rule #5 – Do not start doubtful or out players

Rule #6 – After week 4 start hot players and bench cold players

Rule #7 – Bench players in heavy rain, snow or swirling/gusty winds

Rule #8 – Avoid good defenders and tough defenses

Rule #9 – Use Las Vegas odds to help with close calls

Appendix I Toss-Up Starter Checklist

Checklist for Toss-Up Starter Decisions

1) Go with home team players first (QBs, K and DEF play slightly better at home)

2) Choose those playing in national TV game

3) Choose a player playing in a game you can watch

4) Choose a player playing in the latest game (4 p.m. EST or Sunday Night or Monday Night Football)

Appendix J Acronyms

D	=Doubtful injury status
DEF	=Defense
FF	=Forced fumble
FFPC	=Fantasy Football Players Championship
FG	=Field Goal
FP	=Fantasy Points (based on player's stats and scoring system of league)
FR	=Fumble recovered
HC	=Handcuff (Drafting a player's backup) or Head Coach
IDP	=Individual Defensive Player
INT	=Interception
K	=Kicker
NFFC	=National Fantasy Football Championship
NFL	=National Football League
OL	=Offensive Line
P	=Probable injury status
PPR	=Points per Reception
Q	=Questionable injury status
QB	=Quarterback
RB	=Running Back
REC	=Reception or catch of a pass
SOS	=Strength of Schedule
ST	=Special Teams
TD	=Touchdown
TE	=Tight End
TO	=Turnover (Fumble or Interception)
TP	=Total fantasy points
WCFF	=World Championship of Fantasy Football
WDIS	=Who Do I Start
WR	=Wide Receiver
XP	=Extra Point
YPC	=Yards per Catch

Index

About the Author

Sam "Slam" Hendricks grew up in Lynchburg, Virginia and graduated from the University of Virginia in 1986. He joined the USAF and flew RF4C fighter jets in Germany during the Cold War. He transitioned into the F15E Strike Eagle and earned three aerial achievement medals during combat missions in Operation Desert Storm.

Sam left the Air Force in 1993 to work for McDonnell Douglas as an F15E instructor, a job he has performed for more than 16 years. He and his Danish wife, Birgitte, have spent the last ten years in Europe.

Sam participates in the World Championship of Fantasy Football (WCOFF), National Fantasy Football Championship (NFFC) and the Fantasy Football Players Championship (FFPC) where he has finished 7th and 16th overall the past two years (out of 228 top competitors). He has won numerous league championships in his 20-year fantasy football career. He is a member of the Fantasy Sports Writers Association (FSWA).

Sam has an MBA in Business and a Masters in Personal Finance. His next book (release date May 2011) will be on personal finance and the day-to-day things we can all do to improve our finances.

Lightning Source UK Ltd.
Milton Keynes UK
10 January 2011

165434UK00009B/167/P